BOTTOM DOG

PRESS

HUNGER ARTIST
A Suburban Childhood

Joanne Jacobson

Harmony Series
Bottom Dog Press
Huron, Ohio

Author Photo: Jane Windsor
Cover Design by Ellen Wertheim
Layout by Susanna Sharp-Schwacke

Ohio Arts Council
A STATE AGENCY THAT SUPPORTS
PUBLIC PROGRAMS
IN THE ARTS 40 Years

ACKNOWLEDGMENTS

Like my parents' move to the suburbs, this book has been a labor of love and hope, and I've had the great luck to have been able to count on so many others in writing it.

Stephen Donadio has been a caring, wise colleague for more than twenty years; in publishing "My Father, Reading" in *New England Review* he made my vision of my new writerly voice into something real. The Ragdale Foundation has offered me for the last decade precious quiet and community and focus—and the chance to be taken seriously as a working writer. Ellen Geist, my writing *chevrusa* partner, and Susan Thames both took the time to provide attentive editing at crucial moments in the evolution of this book. Marsha Melnick, Susan Meyer, Sabrina Farber and Ellen Shapiro all read portions of the manuscript and offered encouragement and savvy advice; Patricia Volk, Faye Moskowitz, and Julie D'Acci provided gracious, generous support at crucial points. And my lifelong friend Lucy Childs insisted on the work's potential and gave herself to it, and to me, with nerve and realism.

I have been the beneficiary of a summer faculty fellowship, two sabbatical leaves and funding for writing residencies from Yeshiva University; I'm grateful to Morton Lowengrub, Norman Adler, Fredric Sugarman and David Srolovitz for that essential support. The entire Production staff at YU has tended to my needs for scanned photographs and photocopying with patience and care, frequently going the extra mile to get things out for me quickly. And Joan Haahr has been for a decade and a half my dream colleague at Yeshiva: full-hearted with her time and her loyalty at every stage of my career and my work and my life; family.

And more family: this book's subject and its blood. Richard McCann and I have seen one another through so many difficulties and joys, right to the edge of life: he has been my model writer, my inspiration, my brother. I'm happy that Timi Mayer and Tahl Mayer have also been for so long sharers in my life, companions as well as readers. And all my family in Chicago and Minneapolis and Washington: my nephews and my niece, my brother-in-law, and my cousins; my aunts and uncles; and, especially, my mother and my sister. I am grateful that we continue to find so much in one another. Their support has made remembering and writing a charge that I have tried my best to honor and to treat with respect.

At Bottom Dog Press, Larry Smith made the commitment to this book that has brought it to life—and helped to shape and polish the manuscript in ways that I know have made my work stronger. In her turn, my publicist Meryl Zegarek has provided the confidence in the work and the experience and optimism to bring it to the widest possible audience.

I am grateful to the editors of the following journals, in which earlier versions of some of this work appeared:

"My Father, Reading" first appeared in *New England Review.*

"Prelude" first appeared in *BOMB,* as "American Children."

"Hunger Artist" first appeared in *American Literary Revew.*

Portions of 'Garden Days" first appeared in *Heartlands* as "My Father's Gardens."

"Cheeseburger" first appeared in *Alimentum.*

Finally, Ellen Wertheim has lived with this book since I took my first tentative steps toward writing it; she has unstintingly believed in my writing and in me; she has generously taken time away from her own art to help me at every point along the way. Her contributions are visible not only on the book cover—but on every page of prose. She has taught me that love is what it's all about, language's most needful and cherished occasion.

DEDICATION

For my mother

הֵן עַל־כַּפַּיִם חַקֹּתִיךְ

See, you are engraved
On the palms of my hands

Isaiah 49:16

HUNGER ARTIST: A SUBURBAN CHILDHOOD

PRELUDE

I

In the sweet, lucky June when I was nearly six, my parents turned from the city where they had been children and lovers, and where their own parents had loved them, and hoped for a new beginning. The long years of war and of holding back were behind them. Up Chicago's suburban lakeshore they found a big house on a block carpeted with spring-green lawns and lined with spreading trees; together they took their children there, my sister and me, charged with their appetite for fresh life.

Each time we landed at the front curb in our Studebaker Lark—plain and tan and cumbersome, a relic of the strained years on my father's salary as a medical resident that were now ending—we crossed over to more favored territory. My mother would reach into the back of the car and collect my baby sister, my father would flip his half of the front seat forward so that I could climb out, bending to avoid the thin cloth liner hanging ragged from the metal roof overhead. And the two car doors would bang decisively shut, a few seconds apart, in succession. Our apartment on the north side of Chicago—only ten minutes away—was already shadowed in memory, encircled by dark buildings, while each of the three-story homes on our new block seemed to glow before us on its own dais of emerald grass. Ours had its own name that I practiced saying over and over: Seven Eleven Michigan, Evanston, Illinois.

I was old enough to ride a bicycle, my parents told me—but I chose a little red tractor with pedals instead, low to the solid ground, four wheels steady and even. I rumbled down our wide sidewalk, instantly proficient, as soon as we unloaded the tractor from the trunk of the car. My mother and my father were already on the path of transformation, and I wanted to be with them, in motion, pitching in.

The entire world seemed to lie molten around us, amenable to our presence, inviting us to leave our mark, set in dream time. With gleaming new tools—pronged trowels, hoes, rakes—we opened the earth in our yard, uprooted weeds, collected fallen leaves from the autumn and the spring that had passed just before we arrived, and deposited them in a pile near the garage, where they yielded luxurious mulch. In a miraculous flash, it seemed, we were brought into the presence of excess: the lilies of the valley crowding the ground, loaded with odor; the gigantic, silky peonies flowering all at once, teetering at the tips of tall stalks, crawling with greedy ants; the soft, shallow trail of sticky clippings that accumulated behind my mother when she mowed the grass. My parents were intoxicated by seed catalogs, by their lavish foretelling of possibility. Roses—just pink roses!—came in countless varieties. My mother and father turned the glossy pages at the kitchen table, and breathlessly ripped open their deliveries of seeds and the peat starter sets that would dissolve into the soil as soon as the young plants took root.

I was drawn by the tar trucks that rolled slowly down our street, by the rich, steamy smell that rose from each layer that they laid down. From pits at the core of the planet the tar came before it was spread over the crumbly roadbed and left to congeal. I would close my eyes and breathe deeply, and I'd bend to touch the jet black paste, still sticky and aromatic. The earth's deep, oozing essence was revealed to me just over our curb—shining and drying when it reached the surface. For we had shimmied close to the lapping edge of a bigger universe, I already knew. My mother and my sister and I would walk to Lake Michigan, just two blocks away, the garage door snapping behind us on its fat spring, the alley grinding beneath our thin flip-flops and sticking to the rubber. Along the shore the entire town—newly ours, newly mine—was spread before me. I knew from the shocking chill of the water that clasped my feet beneath the hot air, and from the hazy horizon line drawn across the distant water, that the lake must be a vast thing, connecting me somehow to another place, far away from where I stood.

My mother sowed plants throughout the lawn, calculating what it took to keep everything alive. One of her sprinklers cast a wide, unhurrying arc, leaving a margin of sidewalk that pedestrians passed at an anxious angle, pressed against an invisible wall; two others spun at the farthest corners of our property, drenching the final inches of green that she had measured.

And the seasons began to move, it seemed, to the rhythm of growing and blooming that my own mother set. During our first autumn in the house she sank bulbs at the yellowing border between the grass and her rock garden; in the spring she surrounded the house with a velvety layer of ground cover. In winter she kept a shovel on the front steps, and she drove a straight, certain path through every snowfall, clearing our way to the curb. Through the deepest white, cold and wet, we would make our daily way, in her wake, to the new world.

II

My mother's mother and father seem in old photographs suspended in a force field close to their Chicago house—their motion checked, as though otherwise they were liable to slip beyond the concrete arc of their front stoop and come unanchored. Behind them the mounting bricks of their bungalow frame every image. My grandmother and my grandfather always stand, creating a formal portrait: she in a plain cotton dress and he in a white shirt, freshly pressed pants and polished shoes. They never look at one another, they never hold one another, they never touch. They leave a self-conscious measure of inches between them. Even in their own yard they never take a casual seat on the lawn chairs or the back steps. As a teenager at the start of the twentieth century my grandmother had been sent out of Poland, entrusted to an uncle with a rag trade job in New York and then betrothed to my grandfather, a cigar maker who had fled the Czar's army a few years before. On the South Side of Chicago she and her husband became parents, fed their children through the Depression, sent a daughter and their son to college and then the son to war, and, at the finish of the killing years in Europe, became grandparents. Yet they walked quietly across American ground. In their pictures they offer up an armload of grandchildren as explanation for seeking the attention of the camera.

How different their children were! In the rush of photos they took after the war they love in public, my mother and my father and my uncles and my aunts, rolling with their sweethearts on the grass, in yards and in city parks and on the sand along the Lake Michigan shore. Nothing holds them back, nothing waits to be explained. Nothing is out of bounds for them. Wherever they go, they dispense with shirts, with hats, with long pants. They hang on one another's shoulders, they tangle in each other's hair. Bare backs lean, sweaty and shameless, against bare backs. Their grins flirt with the camera; they know that the world has just been saved for them.

They married and honeymooned, careening fearlessly on skis down mountains of snow. On deep Wisconsin lakes carved by glaciers they rented cabins where pine logs left a resinous, muscular scent in the bedclothes and the bang of screen doors and the grinding crescendo of outboard motors followed their meals. Wives and husbands and young children, more every year—they swam into deep water, stripped down to the barest of fabric, willingly exposed. They posed on aluminum docks that bounced and rang under their running feet.

Around the suburban homes that they bought, evening clung in summer, soft as flannel: warm, gray, dense; pulsing with fireflies. My parents and their siblings cooked in the open, in petroleum bursts of lighter fluid that settled onto the glowing pyramid of coals; later in the tired dark someone would spill a bucket of water into the grill, and a finale of loud steam would rise from the live ashes. Indoors, paper plates were stacked on the kitchen counter, loaded with charred meat pooled in watermelon and spit-out seeds—the leavings of plenty.

My mother's mother passed the afternoon and the day's slow finish on her children's back porches, her nylon stockings rolled down in the heat around her thick ankles, beside a pile of mending collected by daughters and daughters-in-law trying to make her feel useful. American noise beat all around my grandmother—the happy screams of her grandchildren, the slow whining of an automobile squeezing into the last parking spot on the block; a neighbor's surging lawnmower, a barking dog, an impatient mother calling children to bed—and my grandmother continued to sew, hearing nothing.

My grandmother had imagined dance—her daughter would be a ballerina—and she had imagined light and sound, her son on stage, spotlighted, making beautiful music. But in the end she would break my young uncle's violin over his head because of the sounds it made: sounds without promise. And she would curse my cousins for marrying strangers; *goyim* forever to her no matter what tricks of word or ritual they managed to call up.

This country would forever remain to my grandmother an alien destination, to which necessity rather than hope had driven her; where even a brick house of her own and a piano, and enough to eat, and scores of college graduations, couldn't vanquish her aloneness. My grandmother never let down her guard against America, never was not a stranger here herself. "Every Easter the nuns would come to spit on us," was the only memory of her Polish childhood that she offered her American grandchildren, and she meant it as a warning. Even as her appetite for this place's promises continued to run, like a thin, secret aquifer, beneath the conceded surface of the present, my mother's mother balked at what her children dared to expect: to come in close to the unruly, whirring business of life here, and to take hold of it and claim it as their own.

III

My first Fourth of July in the suburbs: white crêpe paper snow drenched the float on which I was outfitted as a penguin under the cloudless summer sky; over me a cord hung with handwritten letters, A-L-A-S-K-A, honoring our newest state and the long, artic reach of the Union. Dazed and sweltering in the wadded, unmelting snow, I struggled to stand upright on my flippers and to breathe through the sagging bill in the heat. But when my parents hurried onto the halted float at the end of the parade route and released me—unpeeling the sodden black mask stuck to my face, and the rest of the heavy costume—I was magically unmolded, and I stepped out of the pile of cloth on the plywood platform and grinned into the sun.

Ownership made my parents zealots, made them pace off their house's long halls with a sense of mission. They rented bulky machines to steam off the old wallpaper, and it came down layer by layer in sweating sheets that my mother and father left to dry in every room while they moved eagerly to the next project. When he got home from work at the hospital, my father would rush through dinner, and the two of them would begin taping on the walls sample paint chips that my mother had collected at the neighborhood hardware store. Visionaries of color and texture and space—they spread carpet remnants in the bedroom upstairs and in the living room below.

Together my parents lugged paint into the house and up the stairs, each can swinging heavily from the wire handle that they shifted from hand to hand as it dug into their soft, unpracticed flesh. Beneath each ridged lid that they pried off, a shimmering layer of oil floated over the silky liquid. My mother or my father would take one of the flat wooden sticks that the hardware store gave away, and begin slowly stirring the mixture until it became a tremulous single thing, luscious and fragrant. Even with the windows open and rotary fans going, the smell of paint rising on those hot days from opened cans and drying on walls, and of turpentine-soaked rags, wrapped everyone in its potent closeness. As each room heated up and the air thickened, my parents steadily unclothed. By the time they finished wiping the day's brushes and leaving them to soak they would be wearing old, ripped shorts and my father's discarded white undershirts. Just so—sticky with paint and sweat, well pleased with what they had done together; at their ease—they would sit out on their back steps, and my mother would rest on my father's stained knees in the gently collecting dusk.

I was forbidden to play in the empty lots near our house, in the construction sites where splintery planks were strewn, studded with nails. Still, in the long, hazy hours of the late afternoon, the neighborhood kids drifted in bunches into the deep craters after the workers had left for the day. Silently each of us would drop, scraping against the rough cement slabs of the foundation until our sneakers sank into mounds of excavated soil. We would fan out and play in the faltering light, spooking one another, throwing our voices around corners, calling out and skipping away, skidding in a chalky barrage of dust and gravel. On the bare concrete walls we imagined the outlines of rooms in which families as yet not known to us—capable of anything—would soon makes lives in our midst.

If the melody of an ice cream truck reached us from the street above we'd race out, nearly overpowering the driver in his white trousers and shirt and the half turban of a service uniform. He would flip a silver lever and throw the freezer doors wide open, one to either side, reaching in as we all shouted our orders. We'd drop the paper wrappers and sit in a row along the curb, each with a twinned Popsicle—clear, icy cherry or grape or banana or blue raspberry—or a creamy Fudgsicle; or an orange Dreamsicle, crystal sherbet whirled into soft ice cream. We sucked and chewed down to the soiled, splintered sticks left in our hands, one final sticky pleasure before our mothers called us home to dinner.

In late August or early September as we played softball, a dull sound began to gather in the field like static, softer than wind, as though the dial on a far-off transistor radio was being gently turned. We looked up and shivered: between us and the high sun a thin cloud was moving in, rolling in low waves. At the edges, dark motes flashed. We paused and stood, watching and listening—not quite afraid but aware of the mysterious presence that had come close to each one of us, moving as we breathed and as our hearts beat in the dimmed light and the soughing air. As the cloud passed, frantic objects became caught in the high mesh backstop and slid, stunned, to the ground where we found them: monarch butterflies stilled on their long annual migration south from Canada to Mexico. The velvet legs twitched when we touched them, the orange and black wings, tinsel-thin, beat with fear in our clumsy, cupped hands, slowly weakening before we realized—too late—what fragile glory we held, already fading in the last of the summer sun.

When my mother and I shopped for the coming year's school supplies, I was finally permitted to give up on last year's crayolas, the remaining stubs and fragments sealed in grimy, frayed paper. I paced the old five-and-ten with its warped, creaking floorboards, trying out plastic rulers in fluorescent colors, reading the raised numbers—inches on one side, centimeters on the other—with my fingertips, like Braille. And for a few intoxicated days the new crayons, with their perfect points, gave off the elemental fragrance of wax and freshly unwrapped paper.

My mother felt it, too: a chill spark of readiness at the end of long, blurred heat. For my October birthday she collected cousins and their parents and grandparents, and drove to where the year's fresh apples had just finished growing. The orchard was laid out in dense rows that closed around us as we entered. Ladders rose into the branches, disappearing in a tangle of growth so ripe that a groping hand would knock fruit, unintentionally, to the ground. I followed the rough rungs upward until the sound of voices grew muffled and distant, until the sky seemed closer, more real, than the earth.

When they found a clearing where the line of trees faltered, my mother and father spread an old army blanket on the nubby dirt, feeling beneath the coarse olive-colored wool for lumps of fallen fruit. On the unraveling satin edge of the blanket they set their heavy items: the plastic jug of cider that they'd purchased at the shop just inside the front gate of the orchard; the nicked styrofoam cooler that they always lugged on picnics. From my perch I could feel the air stir as they passed below with their load of bologna and egg salad sandwiches, carrot sticks and celery, and the birthday cake—white with chocolate frosting, my special request—that my mother had baked. I could hear my parents call in my friends from the trees where they had scattered, and my sister and my young cousins who were playing hide-and-seek. I could see my grandparents lagging behind, making their way hesitantly across the uneven ground strewn with slick, chewed apples.

Above them all I waited in the high trees, where the apples hung in lush clusters. When winter came the squirrels would search out their caches of shriveled fruit, their harsh calculation. But I was not thinking beyond this moment. This was my time of luxurious fulfillment, and I fed at my leisure above the littered earth on my favorites: taut, honey-colored Golden Delicious. I bit into the crisp flesh and let the sweet juice dribble and stick on my cheeks, I let half-eaten fruit fall from my hands as I reached for the next apple, and the next—forgetting hunger and forgetting the bushel baskets that my mother had patiently filled and packed into the trunk of our car, the applesauce and the cobbler whose aroma would linger in our kitchen in the long wake of her labor. For just this day, just these hours, I hung in the sky, in the quiet light of ripeness: this was my birth time.

PART ONE

"This island even exceeds the others in beauty and fertility."
—Christopher Columbus,
Journal of the First Voyage to America, 1492-1493

EVANSTON, 1958:

Me in our new
garden in Evanston.

My sister Anita and me
in our new backyard.

Cousins on our new
back porch, Danny,
me, Howie, Anita, Mark.

Dreaming in Things

In the lustrous afternoons that followed my first school days I bounced in the crackling yellow and red piles of leaves, still pungent with life, that my mother had raked in the back yard next to the garage. I could feel change picking up around me, could smell and hear it: smoke clouding the crystal air as our neighbors' burning leaves popped and hissed in the middle of our street; the rich, sweet fragrance of death. My parents had explained, pointing upward, where those leaves came from, and I assumed that scientists had used ladders and telescopes to follow the trail, tracing the fragile twigs and then the thickening branches high up into the trees. There the leaves hung, they must have discovered—as invisible to the naked human eye, and nearly as distant, as stars in the wide night sky. But after a few fuzzy weeks in first grade I was sent home with a note informing my parents that I needed eyeglasses. And now the world turned suddenly sharp and whole. With my own eyes I saw leaves growing on the trees, and a single leaf carried in the autumn wind newly emptied of heat: the living world set before me in purposeful motion.

*   *   *

My bicycle had pounding, fat balloon tires that I'd use my entire weight to bring to a rough halt. I could feel in the soles of my feet the ragged release of momentum, always just slightly uncertain, rubber softly grinding the pavement. I dreamed of moving up to a racing model with thin, taut wheels. When you squeezed its hand brakes—poised silver wings hanging from the handlebars—you'd instantly sense objects gripping, taking hold, clamping down to a precision stop. The three-speed and its fantasy cousin the ten-speed were palpable advances on the crude forces of the body that bullied bikes up hills and struggled for control over them on the way down. With instruments such as these— vehicles of transformation—I could sail into the universe.

On my first twenty-inch bicycle I swung crazily from one side of the sidewalk to the other, ten years old, crashing in the grass beneath a heap of spinning metal. I'd shove the bike angrily into the back yard, one hand steering the seat beneath the listing wheel. But once I got the hang of it, I would wait for the Number Three bus to pass on the half hour and then push off into the street with a victorious grin, picking up momentum, stopping for nothing. And I wasn't the only one: as soon as breakfast was over, kids on the block would mount bicycles and meet one another near the front curb, swooping in a line down Forest Avenue. Too small for a two-wheeler, my sister waited on the sidewalk, aching for our swiftness. We'd pack tuna salad sandwiches in tight Saran Wrap and take long rides, first maneuvering our way through the neighborhood streets and then breaking free down the lakeshore bike paths, pedaling as fast as our burning calves would let us, daring to let go of the handlebars—taking our chances.

In the shop the bikes were racked in a long line, from sixteen-inchers with training blocks strapped to their pedals to the special models, twenty-eight inches high, that the owner kept in stock. The cavernous room smelled of oil and of new things: rubber and steel, freshly ripped cardboard cartons, and the plastic sheeting that hooded each untried seat. When the door to the street closed behind me, I could barely see to the back of the store with the sun from the picture window strong and glaring. A few display bikes were scattered in the open space at the center, resting on their kickstands among fragments of light thrown on the dark wood by the window and the mullioned door; haloed in the graded brightness. Against the wall all the bicycle wheels were turned in the same direction— shadowed, parallel circles rising and fading into the hazy background. I sensed myself stepping onto a launchpad: as my eyes adjusted to the dimmed light, I saw revealed before me the means of acquiring speed and conquering distance.

I paced the floor, flicking my fingers through the clinking baskets of safety reflectors—red circles and squares and triangles that my father screwed in behind my seat and threaded between the spokes of both wheels—and caressing the leather saddle bags with their narrow straps and their aroma of luxury. Each spring when I wheeled my bike out of the garage, my hopes would reawaken: for multicolored handlebar streamers, for a battery-powered buzzer. When Schwinn released a new color, a creamy forest green with metallic flecks, I longed for it. Then I would need an electric headlight, mark of my freedom to ride at night as well as in day. And then—now—*now* was all there was: ringing my metal ball with a flick of my right wrist and hearing the clear sound trail behind me; seeing my shiny handlebars draw the light; generating my own current.

*   *   *

For the Halloween bonfire kids gathered at Baker Park, around the corner from my house. Our acetate hoods and capes, too flimsy to cut the chill, flickered in the floodlights strung temporarily across the playing field where we huddled—a cluster of store-bought Supermen and Batmen, and homemade ghosts squinting through rough holes in sheets that kept slipping below our eyes. All at once the pile of wooden crates would turn into flame: a living, barely contained thing showering sparks. The firemen poised at the edge of the lit circle would become visible, closing in just slightly at the perimeter, costumed in heavy black, wearing bright, billed hats and carrying slack hoses. All around me features turned on and off in the wild light—flesh and blood, skeletons rippling in glow-in-the-dark silver on black cloth—changing color and form, making me giddy.

Once the days of sharp cold came, men in city uniforms hooked up the fire hydrants and flooded Baker Park to create a block-long skating rink. My mother bought me white leather ice skates, securely laced in two long rows of metal hooks, and showed me how to use the silver turnkey; how to tighten the laces pair by pair of eyelets, up, toward my knees, and how to tie a double knot at the very top.

Ice set over the playing field in an uneven sheet, its surface bumpy with bits of gravel that had mixed into the freezing water. My friends and I skated with abandon, mounting on blades and sailing the hard surface. We'd grab one another's hands to form a human chain and then whip swiftly, trailing a shivery, grinding sound and icy shavings. When a heavy snow was falling we could hardly see one another in the fog of flakes. We could only feel: the elastic pull of bodies, extending invisible into soft whiteness; and the sudden snap that came, powerfully, when the last skater was pulled into the turn. Or we would skate in insular pairs, silently tracing the edge of the ice in long, looped arcs, imagining ourselves performing before a hushed audience at the Olympics or on the set of *Doctor Zhivago*.

We could be anything, really, when we dressed for it. Every kid on the block had a Davy Crockett cap that trailed a coonskin tail in the wind when we picked up speed on our bikes. We had Mouseketeer caps, too, with black, outsize ears, and firemen's hats that teetered on our heads, all rubber bill and dome. At Chanukah my grandfather took the elevated train down to Comiskey Park, at the far side of the city, to buy me a regulation White Sox uniform. Throughout the long winter I'd check the big box under my bed, the clean white jersey and trousers resting under tissue until the weather grew fine. While my teammates ran the bases in shorts and T-shirts, I hovered in the roasting outfield, dreamily fingering the official Sox insignia darned onto my pocket.

After breakfast, my sister would take off the clothes that our mother had chosen for her and begin again, preening in her bedroom doorway—naked except for a chiffon tutu. Anita would sling one arm rakishly to the side, bracing herself in the door jamb, letting the diaphanous skirt—pinker even than her four-year-old skin—hang from the elastic at her waist. Sometimes I'd join her there in my cowboy outfit, in the shirt with its bold stitching and fringes and my stiff jeans. I'd ease my gun in and out of the holster and stroke the plastic bullets that I'd loaded into the slots along my belt.

"Sign in, please," the host of TV's *What's My Line?* would instruct each week as we watched from the living room sofa. Each contestant hoped to stump the show's panelists, lined up in formal eveningwear behind a long, plain desk. Only the contestant—the female grease monkey in her very best dress, the wild snake veterinarian in a sport jacket and a bow tie— knew the truth: *Who am I? What do I do?* Or the panel members would put on elegant masks and try to identify the night's famous Mystery Guest, Bob Hope or Milton Berle.

A simple strip of fabric would render us mysterious as well, potent and unknowable. And then we could play by our own rules, like the masked men whom we knew from comic strips and television: the Lone Ranger, Zorro, and Wonder Woman. Like Clark Kent we were on the alert in the realm of the ordinary, ready to be transformed.

CHEESEBURGER

In my dreams I eat at the B&G, the diner on Evanston's Main Street two blocks up from Lincoln School. When our grandparents visit, my sister and I count on walking over to the B&G with them on Saturday afternoon. "Our treat," my grandmother offers brightly, waving an expansive hand toward my grandfather on the couch in front of the TV and then back toward her own bosom. I follow my grandparents down the sidewalk, counting the left and right turns that lead us to where we are going.

I might go through the motions of accepting a menu from the aproned waitress—propping the cushioned folio on the formica tabletop and turning the heavy, laminated pages—but this is just a gesture, as ritualistic as the moment when I set the closed volume at my place, and as inevitable as my order: a cheeseburger and French fries with a cherry Coke.

Planted at the center of my toasted sesame bun, when it arrives, will be a toothpick wrapped in a twist of colored cellophane, flying a miniature red-white-and-blue American flag. On the thin patty inside, two wavy slices of dill pickle will, I know, be sitting in a thin layer of mustard and ketchup. The fries will be heaped on one side of the plate and a shallow, pleated paper cup loaded with a single serving of cole slaw will be set near the opposite edge. I hold the crusted lip of the ketchup bottle over the plate and tap the upended bottom until thick liquid starts down in a rush, leaving a cold, sweet puddle into which I dip the almost too hot, salty fried potatoes one by one. I let my tongue and my teeth find the greasy meat inside the soft bread, the crunch and tang of the condiments.

I can feel the pillowy plastic of the booth's long seat settling into sticky place around my thighs. When I climb down, I drop to the black-and-white-checked linoleum with a little thump. Above me things are already in motion, coming to a conclusion: the waitress bending down to deliver mints to my sister and me; my grandfather handing the paper slip of our check with a couple of folded bills over the glass counter, high over our heads, to the cashier; the cash register ringing, the metal drawer sliding open and banging shut. The plate glass door gives us a breathy push onto the sidewalk, and the curtain comes down behind us.

Junior Masters of the Universe

My father and mother remembered each spring the fear that hot weather had brought to their parents: the great shadow that polio cast over summer. Just at the time of year when the sun was at its most inviting, mothers and fathers had to forego the beaches that lined the city, for many believed that the mysterious disease that killed and crippled was spread in water. And children were the favored victims of the polio virus. It withered their legs and their lungs, leaving them hobbling in braces; it left them encased in iron lungs, unable ever again to come up for air on their own. My cousins and my friends and I would be among the first in history to have freedom of this.

Not that we gave a thought to our own unfettered movement, or even to our needle-sore arms or the new sugar cubes dotted with miraculous medicine, though it had been only a handful of years since children were being maimed. For we knew little of illnesses that ravaged: tests and inoculations—the promise to repair, to make better—were all that was left of them. And what child could guess from pricks and scratches in the doctor's office the coughing and the disfigurement, and the dying, of tuberculosis and smallpox? Danger itself seemed to have atrophied in our time. When another child on the block came down with chicken pox or with the measles, my mother would intentionally expose my sister and me, inviting the disease into our home, daring it to make us immune. We were the lucky ones, treated to the luxury of risk.

For we were junior masters of the universe. We were promised dominion over the near—our bones and organs, warm as blood—and the far: over revolving solar systems; the mysteries of life itself. The secrets of the world we lived in were steadily revealed to us: on the way to the Dairy Queen, my uncle taught us to count the seconds between flashes of lightning and booms of thunder so that we could know how far away the storm was. I subscribed to *National Geographic*, and my parents helped me decorate my bedroom with the maps and charts that were inserted into every issue: *The Night-Time Sky*, a black field sparkling with clustered stars; *Emerging African Nations;* the wavy-lined *Topography of the Ocean Floor.* Over my doorway we unfolded a long diagram of evolutionary turning-points: the stirrup-shaped stapes bones of the inner ear, characteristic of mammals; the three-toed foot of *therapods,* the three-fingered hand of *tetanurans;* the eye socket of *tethyteras,* pushed forward to near the snout. At the end was a photograph of a paleontologist at work, using a tiny jackhammer to carve mineral deposits from a clutch of fossilized dinosaur eggs—drawing back time's hidden curtain on my own wall.

If I felt like it I could ride my bike to the South Branch of the Evanston Public Library, a corner storefront where the strong light admitted by the plate glass windows sliced the space diagonally, leaving one side shadowed like a domino square. As I shut the door I could feel the street noise being squeezed out behind me; only the breathy turns of swiveling fans disturbed the silence of the big room. In the sunniest spot was the reference section, rows of encyclopedias and dictionaries and atlases enclosed by the stacked wooden drawers of the card catalog. Pressed into the outer walls were dim shelves crowded from floor to ceiling with books.

I slowly worked my way through the *Childhood of Famous Americans* series, books that revealed how Eleanor Roosevelt and Benjamin Franklin and the Wright Brothers came to do important things; how Jackie Robinson and Jim Thorpe and George Washington Carver challenged racial prejudice and became models for young people everywhere. Books about the Secret Service and the FBI also fascinated me. Every single threat to the life of the President of the United States, I discovered, was followed up by federal agents! The vast majority proved spurious, the work of eccentrics seeking attention or of kids in Kansas or Wyoming or Miami who had no idea how seriously their pranks would be taken. A single letter on their typewriter—a cracked *a* or a faint *w*—would often prove their undoing. Only a handful of people in the entire U.S. possessed the artistic skill and the steadiness to engrave the Treasury Department plates from which our paper money was printed! I read, amazed, how one gifted forger managed for years to pass the twenty-dollar bills that he drew by hand.

On the way home from the library I might meet friends at the new Baskin-Robbins store. We'd take paper numbers from the dispenser near the front door and join the noisy line jostling past vats of ice cream laid out in freezers under domed glass. Displayed before us in block letters on the back wall were the multitudinous terms of sweet, chill possibility and I was steadily learning them, coming to know them all: *JAMOCA ALMOND FUDGE; CHOCOLATE MINT CHIP; FRENCH VANILLA; ROCKY ROAD.*

*　　　　　　　　*　　　　　　　　*

My pets were proof of my jurisdiction, down to matters of life and death. I poured the two goldfish that I'd won at a neighborhood fair out of the plastic bags in which they swam, like party favors, into an ovoid, round-lipped bowl. When I saw one floating belly-up on the water's surface just a few days later, I scooped it into a flowered cup from my sister's tea set and flushed it down the toilet. On a card table near the window I kept miniature turtles that I bought for fifty-nine cents each at Walgreen's. With the corner of a wooden ruler I demonstrated for my friends how to roust the turtles from the island at the center of their molded bowl where they huddled, the size of half dollars, under stiff green plastic palm trees. My friends and I spoke pig Latin together, rearranging the parts of words so fast that adults could barely follow our conversations: "Urtle-tay! Im-sway! Ast-fay!" we commanded as we pushed my turtles around the bowl, tapping their pointy tails with the ruler, delivering cruel pokes to the tiny back claws that desperately paddled the shallow water.

Out of a void of illegible shapes and colorlessness we brought forth art from Paint-by-Number sets and packets of Venus Paradise pencils. We built birdhouses and jewelry boxes from kits in which popsicle sticks were rationed with instructions for constructing walls and shelves. Around my bed, stacks of Lincoln Logs rose from the textured vinyl sheet that my mother placed wherever I worked, the pitched green roofs balanced at the highest spots. The emptied canister would echo if I snapped my fingers against it or blew softly inside. Using smaller logs and flat planks, I engineered doorways and windows, neatly finishing off each house or office building that I raised nervously until things started to teeter. Off to the side I added a Tinker Toys playground, a maze of wooden dowels and spools. Cans of gritty Play-Doh gave off the aroma of something yeasty, ready to be kneaded and to rise. Bright Cootie insect legs hung like bobby pins, in primary colors, from the thin insert that lined the cardboard box. With his fused pair of feet, his flattened disks of ears and little black plastic eyebrows, Mr. Potato Head waited for us to bring him to life.

The errant particles of the universe seemed to gather in my room like magnetic filings. I unloaded assortment packets of postage stamps over my bedspread and a cloud of paper fluttered slowly down, settling in soft clumps, spilling the entire globe like a can of confetti on the quilted fabric. Many of the stamps—triangular likenesses of tropical fish, exotic birds and butterflies—came from places I had never heard of, from island countries too small to be included in any of the books in which I mounted them: the Maldives, the Seychelles, Mauritius, Fiji. I practiced saying the names out loud, savoring the flavor of distance and authenticity: *Gabon, Togo, Deutsche Post; Magyar; Eire.*

At the stationery store in downtown Evanston, I climbed the worn stairs to the mezzanine where the philatelic department was sandwiched under a low ceiling and pored over the glassine envelopes, the mint blocks and the first-day covers that were locked in long cases. If business was slow, the old man who worked there would pull out the specialty items that I could never afford—a nineteenth-century special-delivery postmark; a rare partial strike on an airmail envelope—or demonstrate how to pick up the stamps with tweezers so that the delicate gum backing and the perforated edges would not be marred. At home my collection was lined up on a bookshelf in big binders that left space for each year's new issues: glossy renderings of the Aswan High Dam and of the Peace Bell at the UN's Dag Hammerskjold Plaza in New York; the Twelve Tribes of Israel; U.S. commemoratives featuring state flowers, famous baseball players, a Kansas sunflower glowing gold against a black background; exotic half-cent denominations, mail from a barely imaginable time. The white pages turned heavy and wobbly as they filled with mounted stamps—each stamp neatly sealed and labeled, anchored quietly at the ordered center of the world.

*   *   *

At our thresholds, dogs stood: clawing at screen doors, impatient to have the run of their territory, barking at strangers. I could close my eyes and trace—in *dog*—a single tremulous line from one corner of the block to the other, from the Lehmans' miniature poodle, forever being clipped and fussed with, down to the Rosmans' little brown dachshund, and every few households in between: the Murphys' velvet Weimaraner, Geneviève (Mrs. Murphy was a French war bride); Alaska, the Stewarts' lush malamute, and the Nelsons' slobbery English bulldog, George. Next door to us, the Landfields' basset hound Jack lived. "Don't you know the difference between dogs and people?" my mother cried out the kitchen window to my sister when she discovered Anita sharing a cherry popsicle through the back fence with Jack. His fat tongue, practically the only thing about him that didn't hang to the ground, was aimed precisely through one of the diamond-shaped openings in the chain-link fence. Neither of our mothers knew that Ellen Rosman and I had been helping ourselves from the knee-high sack of Milk-Bones in the Rosmans' basement, pretending that we liked the hard, rough little biscuits, so dry that they had to be soaked for long minutes in our saliva before we could gnaw on them. Kid and dog, inside and outside, we passed back and forth until nowhere was out of bounds.

My parents on the road.

MOTEL

At the end of our street a big *Sinclair* sign loomed with its brontosaurus over two gas pumps planted on a concrete island. The aroma of motion felt close in the machines there, as my friend Faith Vilas's father cheerfully waited on his customers — unscrewing the cap on a gas tank, slipping in the angled silver nozzle; wiping a windshield with his long squeegee, stretching to reach the high middle zone of glass, gently dabbing a soft cloth to finish. Slick pools of oil congealed near the pumps, and grease-soaked rags were hung from the rims of the industrial drums that Mr. Vilas used as trash cans. Another dirty red cotton rag would be dangling from his back pocket, and I could smell the oil heating up and drying into the cloth, the rich work of the sun saturating the air. Mr. Vilas always gave each of us a hug and then a dime for the pop machine in the garage, and Faith and I would take our sweating bottles back into the office and stretch easefully across the ripped vinyl chairs scattered near the entrance. The neatly folded rectangles of road maps hanging from the office walls inside — *CHICAGO AREA; ILLINOIS; INDIANA; MICHIGAN; WISCONSIN* — made this feel like the right spot from which to start off for just about anywhere. My parents always filled up at Mr. Vilas's Sinclair station before we left town; from the backseat my sister and I could see him waving good-bye to us in the rearview mirror.

On long rides my mother navigated. We'd first coast the lakeshore, boundary between our newly spacious destiny and the destiny of our grandparents on their cramped blocks at the far end of the city. Whenever they joined us, my mother's mother or my father's father and mother would slip into the back seat of the car without a word. If we all emptied out at Stuckey's or Howard Johnson's for cinnamon rolls slathered with sweet, sticky icing, or for ice cream mounded into chilly stainless steel bowls, the anxious smell of mothballs lingered behind them. But my mother and father were ready for motion, and they sailed up concrete ramps onto the roads that unwound across the Illinois state line. My father drove. Next to him in the front seat my mother would twist to check her lipstick in the rearview mirror. She unfolded the flopping pages of the maps—routing and rerouting alternatives to the dotted lines that indicated highways still under construction when Rand McNally went to press—and plotted our way home.

Toward the end of every afternoon on overnight trips, my mother and father would shift restlessly on the wide front seat and begin their search for a motel. "Slow down," she would caution him as a neon hulk rose around a bend, spelling out *EVERGREEN COURT* or *DAY'S END* or *THE GALENA MOTEL*, in the old Illinois lead mining town, home of Ulysses S. Grant. We'd pull tentatively into the opening of a long driveway while the two of them assessed the place from a discreet distance: the kinds of families clustered around the swimming pool; the condition of the screen doors dotting the low slung block.

My mother would signal for silence with a waved hand, and cock her head out the window for some indication of whether or not we should stop here for the night. If she gave the go-ahead we would make our way along the gravel drive to the door marked *OFFICE,* where the car would crunch to a stop and my father would get out, taking a loud stretch and depositing his sunglasses on the dashboard. He would open the screen door and let go carefully to prevent it from slamming behind him. A little bell would sound as he crossed the threshold. We could hear my father from the car, making the night's reservation, as my sister and I pinched one another or made faces in the rear view mirror, letting loose after being cooped up for so long, while my mother began to gather the paper cups and gum wrappers that had accumulated around us. My father would return with a heavy metal key hanging from a plastic tree or a grimy snowman, and sometimes my mother would take the key for a quick look at our room before she nodded again to my father and let us out of the car.

Somehow our motel rooms seemed to me more *ours* than our own house, specially prepared as they were for our arrival.

Across the toilet seat a white sanitary strip was always stretched tightly. My sister and I raced to break the seal and to peel off the paper caps pinched on the lip of the drinking glasses. An ice bucket would be left out on the bathroom sink for us to fill from the noisy, grinding dispenser down the hall. I thrilled to life in such compact, insular quarters, reduced to two big beds and one cabinet, to a single water tumbler and one suitcase apiece. At every motel we got off to a new start, with the smell of air freshener still lingering over a neatly framed expanse of linoleum.

Along the stoop outside the door to our room an assortment of metal chairs would be strewn, red and yellow and green fading from the sun, rust collecting where the paint had chipped. My sister and I would drag the chairs, scraping against the concrete, and arrange them in a little circle. If we were lucky, our parents would give in to our pleading for ice and Coke or Dr. Pepper from the vending machine in the office, and we would ease into the shallow ridges of hot metal on each seat, rocking back and forth on the heavy runners, clutching the icy cans against our stinging skin.

Between the motel and the road there would be a swimming pool surrounded by a chain-link fence and, around the fence, a sparse, badly cared for lawn. When we were ready, we would all change into bathing suits and make our way barefoot over the scratchy grass. My father would hold my sister and me over the edge of the deep end of the pool and release each of us, squealing, while my mother napped on a chaise lounge in his lengthening shadow. Over and over we dropped, sinking in the murky chlorine and then rising to the light. As I broke the surface of the water I could hear the busy road that had delivered us to this shore, and smell the dust raised by cars whizzing past. And finally my mother would gaze off into the distance, one hand held up against the strong sun that was beginning to flatten everything in sight. She would unfold the stack of cheap, nubby white towels printed with the motel's name that had been readied for us in our bathroom. She would stretch out her arms and I would step in and stand, shivering, while she laughed and she spun me and wrapped me snug. I could feel my upturned face giving up moisture to the heat-loaded air, my skin baking dry, smooth and tight as a stone.

Grandpa Meyer, my mother, Grandma Blanche,
Grandma Yetta, my father, Lake Michigan.

Grandpa Meyer, Grandpa Ben, Grandma Yetta, my mother, my
father, Grandma Blanche, and their grandchildren, Chicago.

My parents at the University of Illinois.

My parents' engagement photo.

PART TWO

"… he had as yet no education at all. He knew not even where or how to begin."

—Henry Adams,
The Education of Henry Adams

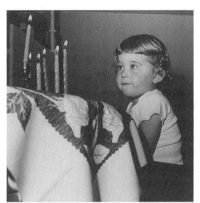
My third Chanukah.

FAMILY TREES

Our Sunday School assignment, at synagogue, is to draw a family tree. Begin with our parents and our grandparents and go back. I picture luxurious linden trees like the one in our front yard, growing in reverse: down into the dark earth where things started; to a blurry, far-away village. The branches arch high over our block of Michigan Avenue, forming a canopy over the parked cars and the fire hydrants.

Our teacher suggests that we interview members of our family. I ask my grandmother, "What did we do in Europe?" She gives me a blank look. *What did your father do, in Poland?* I ask, again. My grandmother's broken English is steadily retreating with age. She reads only the Yiddish newspaper. She says something in a low voice about driving, and draws circles with her hands in the air, turning wheels, pulling an imaginary load over the flattened carpet that has covered her living room floor for as long as I can remember. She carries her cupped hands meaningfully to a spot near the sofa—first sliding them quickly along the rug then lifting them and opening them, dumping something on the ground. Seeing that I don't understand, she shakes her head and gets up, lumbering down the hall to her kitchen.

PONY EXPRESS RIDER, I print in black magic marker on the form that was handed out in class, in the blank spot for my maternal great-grandfather. And I continue upward, filling in "doctor" and "lab technician" and "accountant" and "housewife" for the members of my family whom I have personally met, my parents and my grandparents. For the rest I depend on intuition, on words and fragments I've caught over the years from conversations not necessarily meant for my ears—memories and complaints, the pinched residue of survival; food and shelter and love and hate—and from what I know: "chef" and "architect" and "engineer"; "bookkeeper" and "gardener."

At a holiday dinner I unfurl my little banner tied with black ribbon. I've traced our family back to biblical times, to the elite in the Holy Temple of Jerusalem. Our principal, Mrs. Adler, explained to us that we could hear in our family names ancient stories: those of us with last names like "Cohen" were descendents of the high priests; the ancestors of those named Levy or Levine or Levin—my mother's maiden name—had served as assistants to the priests. Mrs. Adler asked all the Cohanim and the Levites to raise their hands, and I was pleased to see that only Dana Cohen outranked me. But now, over dessert, my mother and my aunts tell me that my grandfather was actually Meyer Hershkovitz before he arrived in the U.S. and was rushed through Ellis Island by immigration officials who changed all the Jewish names that they had trouble pronouncing.

My father stares darkly at the words "Burton Jacobson, MD" on the family tree. Extra space has been left on the tree for information about our parents' activities during the Holocaust. On the dotted lines below my father's name I have filled in: "Nothing." I know that he did not fight in World War II, that he was classified 4-F because he is severely nearsighted. "Nothing?" he is starting now to rage; "Nothing? Do you think that wars are fought from nothing? Our work in the munitions factory was essential to the war effort."

My Sunday school teacher is a World War II veteran who experienced the Holocaust firsthand. He was just out of high school when he was drafted—not so very much older than us, he says, gesturing toward Gary Rosen and Stuart Kellman in the front seats. Mr. Zwick brings to class some of the items that he collected in Europe during the war and spreads them across his desk for us to look at: a canteen, a couple of hollow shell casings, and a stained handkerchief. A stark Iron Cross dangles a tail of shredded ribbon that Mr. Zwick fingers and straightens out absentmindedly as he recalls in his soft voice the skeletons that he witnessed stumbling out of the barracks in the camps.

A lot rests on us: our teachers inform us that we are the future of the Jewish people. Aging survivors of the camps, they strain to make us understand that America and Israel are miracles in our time, that modern Hebrew is the language of redemption, and the suburban prosperity that we take so gracelessly for granted—dumping half-full containers of chocolate milk into the garbage in the middle of class!—is a gift of life that they could never have dreamed during their own childhoods in Poland. Behind Mrs. Tali's back we whisper each other's Hebrew names and snicker at the clunky foreign sounds loaded down by echoes from the Bible and the shtetl: Rivka, Reuven, Malka, Moshe.

We receive subscriptions to the monthly *World Over*. On the back cover of every issue is a full-page cartoon story revealing the hand of Jews in important and unexpected places. Who would have guessed that the Golden Gate Bridge—spectacularly spanning the San Francisco Bay in a double frame on the back of World Over—was designed by a Jew? Or that a Jew thought up Esperanto? In one frame we see an introspective looking figure in wire-rimmed eyeglasses and a trim beard, pondering the lack of communication among different peoples of the world; in the next we see him writing out his visionary idea; in the final frame we learn of the reluctance of people around the world to adopt a universal language.

I shut my lips tight in the Lincoln School Christmas concert when we come to the words on our song sheet: "The little Lord Jesus asleep in the hay." Are Jews forbidden, I wonder, from speaking aloud that exotic, fearsome name? At Girl Scout camp I'm assigned to bunk with four girls from Catholic school who insist during a long rainstorm that I learn to recite the rosary. I can hear water pouring through the trees, seeking a vulnerable spot in the fabric stretched around us, as I finger the little beads and rehearse the lines with them: *Our father who art in heaven/ Hallowed be thy name/ Thy kingdom come, thy will be done/ On earth as it is in heaven.* Could I slip over an invisible threshold, and turn into a Christian? When I ask this of my Hebrew teacher, she calls me silly and gives me her back.

Because of us, Jewish National Fund forests are advancing up the hillsides of Israel, holding the line against erosion and holding off the vast, eddying desert. At springtime we make contributions on Tu Be'Shvat, the holiday of trees. We purchase little green stickers shaped like leaves for a dime apiece and lick the adhesive backs and fix them on glossy drawings that each of us has been issued. When we have hung twenty leaves from the branches in our drawing, we can name our own tree and receive a personalized certificate from the still new State of Israel.

I imagine visiting my own grove in Israel, the result of years of Tu Be'Shvat purchases. I picture myself consulting a large map in a ranger's station on which the coordinates of my planted trees have been plotted, and wandering among the trunks hung with plaques bearing the names of my deceased relatives: my aunt Esther, whose husband provided us every year with Schwinn bicycles from his shop; my great-grandmother Freitka, in Poland, who died when her youngest daughter was born, before my grandmother could know her; my father's aunt Anne, for whom I was named. My grandfather, Meyer Hershovitz, who lost his name, and my great-grandfather Chaim Carmel who drove a dairy wagon through the thin light of dawn, leaving milk and butter on village stoops.

DRUGSTORE

I was always hungry, always wanting more. Around me the stage-sets of desire shimmered, and I haunted them: scuffed toy stores and five-and-tens where Snickers and Hershey bars lined the shelves below the cash register and a mosaic of gum packets—Juicy Fruit, Chiclets, Dentyne; Bazooka Joe bubble gum—was laid out in yellow and green and red and pink. In warm weather I could see the Turtles, sweating clumps of chocolate and nuts and raisins sealed under plastic wrap just out of reach, next to the boxes of Whitman's Samplers with their stitched hieroglyphic borders. At the Rexall drugstore I stood at attention, riveted by trays of freshly roasting cashews dipping flushed and fragrant over the long soda counter and slowly righting themselves like carnival Ferris wheels. I stalked the aisles, my appetite ignited.

Like a wolf I hunted, prowling and stealing to eat. I plucked potato chips from display hooks, spiriting the crackling bags out the door; I helped myself among the cloudy rows of fudge bars and popsicles that lay in a fog of condensation in the deep freezer. The revolving door pressed and turned me onto the street as I held my fragile, melting spoils close.

Every day I returned after school for more of what moved me, at the drugstore and at the five-and-ten; at Just for Fun Toys. The darkly wrapped M&M's and Hershey Bars and the peppermint patties sealed in silver foil waited in the weakening light of late afternoon—too much for me to bear. The cosmetics counter was piled high with elegant gold and black boxes of Jean Naté bath powder and toilet water, too much, with their stiff edges, for me to fit into my pocket. I let the sweet, heavy scent that hung in the air move me while my hand reached, like a separate entity, for the bright matchbooks stacked on a nearby counter, touched them, fit them into the fleshy ridges of my moist palm. And the beckoning goods of the Christian seasons: Advent calendars with their mysteriously shut flaps and ornate illustrations, the starry dots burning in the pitch sky, the cardboard figures in robes and crowns and haloes; the fuzzy yellow cotton Easter chicks, soft as silk—precisely the size of my enclosing fist.

"It's enough now," my mother insisted after the drugstore lady caught me and I pushed on, continuing my litany of confessions at home. I forced my mother to return to every store where I'd been a thief, making widening circles from the drugstore and the dime store nearby to the little neighborhood grocery and even Mr. Vilas's gas station, where I'd taken the plastic windshield scraper that was conveniently stowed in a corner on the sloping dashboard of my mother's own car. At each store I held the door open for my mother, making sure that she followed me inside. I told each owner what I had taken, what my mother hadn't noticed. And finally she refused me. "It's over," she announced roughly on our way home one afternoon, still bewildered but moving now into anger. "You've paid for what you did. I'm not going with you any more. I mean it."

What did I want from my mother, what savage penance did I hope to exact from her unwilling presence? Stripped to the bare essentials of need after months alone in the woods, Henry David Thoreau nearly succumbed to the urge to seize a passing woodchuck at Walden Pond and to eat it raw. No less was I driven by the animal cravings with which I had been let loose in the world. I listened from the brink of devouring for the low, guttural voice of satisfaction—a gulp perhaps like a frog's. Or for my mother's voice, telling me what to do.

Nineteen Sixty-Three

I

On Tuesday mornings at precisely 10:30 a sinewy thread of sound—testing our municipal defense system—uncoiled from an unknown point, over and over, for a forever-long five minutes. No matter what I was doing when the whining began, I looked up, expecting the sky to deliver disaster: lightning reaching wildly down for us, or nuclear war. I waited silently for the worst. For the air to become unbreathable; for some blast to pulverize us in its pounding wake.

Or for tornado warnings: the sick yellowing of the hot, wide prairie sky in August, the living world brought to an anxious standstill; the siren's long rise and fall piercing the still air and hovering with cruel patience. My mother and father would gather my sister and me in the basement until a tinny voice announced over our transistor radio the all-clear for Cook County. That night we would see families like ours on TV—fathers and mothers huddled in driveways with arms wound tightly around their children's shoulders, staring in disbelief at their dismembered houses and at couches leaking stuffing on oddly intact front lawns. Camera shots of funnel clouds hanging belligerently over fields would be interspersed with images of roofless trailer homes shorn open like the cut-away displays of Navaho hogans that we built from cardboard and construction paper in shoeboxes at school.

We saw in *The Weekly Reader* photographs of farmers and their wives staring from behind sunglasses as the deadly mushroom cloud rose over the New Mexico desert, and pictures of London families crouched and frightened in dark air raid shelters during the Blitz. It seemed perfectly possible that we might be next on the world's calendar of catastrophe. I always counted to sixty when I heard a siren, allowing one full minute for the arrival overhead of war planes or for the start of the atomic blast. I was mystified by my parents' refusal to build a bomb shelter in our basement storage room even after I had collected sample blueprints at City Hall for their perusal. It was only after hours of digging a uselessly shallow pit with a friend in the empty lot across the alley that I gave up stockpiling toilet paper and cans of tuna fish, filched one by one from kitchen cabinets. My father cut short our discussion with a dismissive laugh: *Why would we* want *to be the only living human beings left on the planet?*

II

I had nearly reached home at lunchtime when I saw Mrs. Davis at the top of her flight of front steps. It was late November—on the box of lawn next to the Davises' driveway the last leaves had been left unraked in the chill air—but Mrs. Davis was sitting outside, right on the cement, in a pair of print cotton pedal pushers and a thin blouse. I could see her from the end of the block, scanning in the direction from which we were coming, from school; as we drew closer I could hear her television thudding loudly through the closed living room windows. "Kids—oh—*kids*," she said, catching sight of her son Robby and me. We were already pausing on our way up the walk, sensing something unfamiliar, emotional electricity, ahead. Mrs. Davis held out her arms wide and grabbed us with hungry tightness. "Oh, kids," she said again, as we both squirmed, "President Kennedy has been shot."

In our kitchen, three doors down, my mother was holding an emptied can over a saucepan on the lit stove, her entire body tuned to the tense, droning announcements coming from the radio in the dining room. When she saw me she looked down and began to stir soup without a word. She ladled the soup into a bowl for me, and I ate. The Landfields' basset hound barked through the neighboring fence, a bus rumbled by, and still neither my mother nor I spoke. All along our block, front doors opened at the end of the lunch hour and women stood for a long last moment with the same television voices blowing at their backs—

checking across the street with one another, reluctant to release their children into the suddenly changed world.

Barely an hour later Mrs. Davis's son Robby knocked on the door of Miss Allen's sixth grade classroom and quietly made the announcement. From my desk in the row next to the playground window I remembered how, only a couple of weeks before, Robby and his older brother Jeff had broken the glass box in the first floor corridor and set off the Lincoln School fire alarm. Our gym teacher had lined up the whole class in shorts and T-shirts at the center of the vast, varnished blond floor and marched us onto the sidewalk along Main Street, where the alarm bell, pulsing through the school's stone walls, and the speeding fire engines turning the corner with long whines had brought weekday traffic to a halt. Robby trailed Jeff and the principal, Mr. Nelson, from class to class the next day, apologizing. He had held resentfully back, dragging his shoes, leaning against the blackboard while his older brother and Mr. Nelson spoke to us about the seriousness of what they had done. A chalky residue of math equations had clung to Robby's navy striped shirt when they turned and went out the door. But now Robby was before us again, hands hanging stiff at his side, mouth opening wide and helplessly shutting — disorder's frighted messenger, loosed from his mother's mourning embrace.

III

I taught myself to whistle on my way home from Hebrew school. Each week autumn sliced the light a little more thin in the hour between afternoon and evening when we were freed from class. Waiting together for the Number Two bus down Ridge Avenue, Lilyan Shapiro and I flirted awkwardly with Roger Bailey and David Lehrman. On the high sidewalk we giggled while they dug at the trim edges of the sodded lawn with their heels. But when I got out at Main Street to transfer to the Number Three, heading east toward the lake, I would be alone on the darkening corner. While the light lasted I would make a game of reading the make and model of each approaching car from its front grille and the shape of the headlights flashing past at rush hour. When a car slowed I'd check the metal letters over the rear bumper: Chevrolet Malibu; Lincoln Continental; Dodge Dart; Ford Falcon. As I stood by myself at the intersection, shifting from arm to arm my massive biology book and my paperback Hebrew dictionary, dusk turned ever more quickly into night, and the sequence of green and yellow and red above me beamed more deeply into the darkness. Whenever another bus passed I shivered in its dim, spewing wake, hoping for the bus to stop and leave someone to wait alongside me.

No more did I feel I could tell my fear to my parents than I could explain to anyone how my whistling began or how it was done: how my tongue rose and flexed, soft flesh probing, tightening—a mix of force and gentleness—against the solid enamel of teeth, as my lips made an opening and I breathed perfect sound through them. I played piano and violin in the school orchestra but I discovered then that I must be my own truest instrument, for I could break the gloom as I waited with the music I made. The Schubert sonatas that pitched clumsily under my fingers on keys and strings turned lilting, vibrato, in the chilly air as I stood alone, searching out in the distance the high, far apart headlights of the bus pushing closer in the line of cars. My cheeks pulsed with a mysterious certainty. Only when a figure rose out of the dark would I become embarrassed by the private passion of my crystal melody and turn quiet.

Soon the bus would arrive, its doors parting with a hydraulic hiss. I would mount the rubber tipped stairs, straining from the street below the curb with my load of books and fatigue, shuffling to find a dime and dropping it into the ringing fare box that the driver turned with a handle by his side. The bus glowed on its sure path from stop to stop down Main Street. I would settle into a warm seat and let myself be cocooned against the fogged windows, surrounded by adults in their buttoned coats calmly reading folded evening papers as they headed home. And though I had clear instructions from my parents to let the bus take me on its long circuit around the neighborhood so that I could be dropped off at our corner, I could feel my rising hunger and the temptation to get off and take a shortcut home.

Was I whistling that night when I hopped down from the last high step into the dark? The bus made its booming turn and left me standing in silence on a side street. From each weakly lit intersection that I crossed, the long blocks stretched away into nothingness. Houses and trees and lawns dissolved—was that Hinman Avenue or Judson?—as I glanced nervously to my right and my left. Was that Kathy Darling's house, that yellow wooden porch barely catching the edge of the streetlight? I seemed to be sailing—alone again—down a long corridor, too black for shadows.

Out of the dense blur the footsteps slipped, like a knife cleanly splitting canvas: a breach abruptly swelling, damage already done. His hand was over my mouth, his arm jamming my back like a blunt instrument, aiming me into the alley. A rank animal smell rose from garbage packed into loosely lidded containers just a head shorter than I was: aluminum cans that rang when gravel spit against them from under his heavy shoes. I knew that sound, and the muffled scratch of my jacketed body sliding in dirt, and the faint buzz of low power lines above me as I lay below his kneeling body. And the sound of a zipper harshly slit open; and breathing, rough and short. But not that voice — warning me that if I made a single sound he would hurt me — and not that hand, following my ribbed knee socks to my knees, reaching for the neat folds of soft cotton that I felt with my fingertips in the top drawer of my dresser every morning before school. The darkness hardened dully around me, I lay at the heavy, airless bottom of it, pinned and muffled, as he wriggled against me. Behind us was someone's garage and someone's back yard, someone's swing set and jungle gym, someone's bike left out, unlocked, for the night, someone's house. But I was very far away, no longer me, a part being fitted by a stranger, sealed in a glass jar.

And then — the glass cracked. New footsteps parachuted in, scattering stones; sound-shapes bloomed. The body above me lurched upward, and the torn, gelatin darkness was whole again as he stumbled and fled. *Are you alright?* A new voice came in overhead, as though the channel had come unscrambled. Different hands were reaching down, standing me on my wobbling legs like an injured doll. *Where am I?* He steered me gently over the littered passageway and into the phosphorescent ring of a streetlight. I turned in a slow circle and saw that I was half a block from home.

Walking toward our front door I could see my mother in the dining room, slipping out of view and reappearing, checkered in the French windows as she counted out forks and knives and spoons at each place around the table. Four plates, four napkins, four glasses. *We must be waiting for Daddy to come home for dinner tonight,* I thought. My sister was shadowed in blue TV light, probably using the extra time to watch one more episode of *Road Runner.* I turned the doorknob slowly, unsure what I ought to say about my trip home. Or whether I should say anything at all. The lights before me seemed to be slowly brightening, the figures taking shape on a stage, curtains parting. I imagined my parents standing at the center, folded together into a little V that opened toward me. They were asking where my glasses had gone, if I had dropped them, why I hadn't picked them up, how I could see. I didn't want to see; I didn't want to hear either, or to answer. I took a step back on the dark stoop, not even bothering to squint, taking in the curious effect of light gently seeping yellow fuzz from window frames, whistling softly to myself.

But my glasses had betrayed me. I opened the door and came inside, I was forced to speak. And my mother took charge in an instant. From the living room couch I could hear her in the kitchen, wielding the phone with fierce calm. She was calling my father, she was calling the police, she was opening the front door and letting all of them in. They were dark and large and blank; life-size cartoon characters tilting stiffly toward me. One of them went back to the alley for my glasses. Suddenly he came into focus before me, a man with a blue hat resting on his bent arm and a brass badge pinned to his rumpled shirt. He was asking me questions: *Can you tell me what he did to you? Could you see what he looked like?*

I was a child, I was my parents' first baby. I was their first great dream: imagined and brought to loved life, transplanted with them to this big house on this broad, long street. When the thunderstorms came and we were driving, so small beneath the booming sky, my father would find me in the rearview mirror and tell me that a car is always the safest refuge from lightning: the rubber tires provide grounding. I wanted my father to explain now to these strangers: *This is what happened. Everything is fine. Our daughter is fine.* But my father stared at me, vexed as a stranger himself, alone in a strange place. He took off his thick glasses and, without looking, wiped them on his shirt; he used both hands to put them back on and he stared hard again, as though the damage might come suddenly to the visible surface. He took a slow look around him, at the living room furniture and the hallway and the mumbling television. He hardly seemed to know where he was.

Father! Isaac called out, curious, as they climbed together, carrying kindling. Abraham's heart shook with his secret: the voice, the directions; the extravagant promises for the future. Here I am, Abraham soothed his son as they made their way together up the unfamiliar path. And—here I am, Abraham promised again, as he finally unbound Isaac and set the shaking child loose. Isaac rubbed his wrists where the crisscrossed cord had dug into the tender skin, and looked up at his father in confusion. Abraham stood silent, dazed and agitated, with the brush tripping him and the voice gone: his child's life had been spared, he knew, but he had let the boy be put in the way of danger.

At the police station my mother and I waited together on scuffed folding chairs. My mother stood first when my name was called, and she tried to take my hand. But I was inside myself, a silent eleven-year-old witness, shaking my head— NO—as I walked with my mother and the police detective, as the blinds rose and the five figures in line-up stared out at nothing, at me waiting invisible in the dark at the bus stop— NO—I did not know any of these men. Adults were buzzing around me: my mother and the police, and the school nurse when I returned that afternoon to school. I waited with the nurse outside the principal's closed door while my mother spoke with him too quietly for me to hear, and then my teacher Miss Allen came to take me back to my desk, fourth from the front in the row closest to the window.

Later Mr. Nelson came to our class to announce as I watched out the window that a student from our school had been attacked in the neighborhood at dinner time, and that we should all try to be home before dark and always be alert and extra careful. I could feel the other students' curiosity rising, and their alarm, as they fidgeted and murmured. I was just barely aware of the wheezing, whistling voices of grown-ups—the warning principal, my echoing teacher. Outside, I could see, the sky was preparing to storm, dark clouds silently massing and drawing closer to the earth where I was planted in my seat.

THE NARROW BRIDGE

"The entire world is a very narrow bridge. The main thing
is to have no fear."
— Rav Nachman of Bratslav

My parents purchased their own soil testing kit so they could
measure what they had on their land and plan for it. They
showed me how to take samples in the backyard with little
wooden spoons that we unpacked from sterile wrappers, how
to dole out the bits of soil into glass vials and mix each one with
a different chemical from the kit. Sometimes the contents could
be identified by the colors that they turned, or we'd dip one of
the litmus paper strips that came in a vial of their own, to check
the ph level. Each plant thrived under particular conditions—
acid or alkaline, dry or moist; loving sunlight or shade—and
my parents meant to find the right place for every living thing
that they grew.

One Saturday afternoon when I was alone in the house, I
brought the soil testing kit up from the basement where my
parents stored it in a cabinet with the bleach bottles and the
canisters of toxic cleanser. I unpacked the glass beakers and flasks
inside and arranged them, smallest to large, in rows on the
kitchen table. I studied the printed instructions for assembling
the Bunsen burner and mounted it on its wire stand, set over
fire. Every test tube of chemicals had its own slot in a steel rack.
I loosened the stoppers and poured a sample from each one into
the long- necked flask. I opened the round tin of solid kerosene,
and lit the fuel beneath the Bunsen burner with a wooden match
from a drawer next to the sink. I stirred the mixture in the flask

with a clinking glass rod as it slowly heated on the kitchen table and changed color, to a deep, gorgeous orange.

When it exploded, the orange liquid shot up without warning in a soundless rush through the narrow neck of the flask and squirted onto the kitchen walls and ceiling, where it clung in gooey patches to the sunshine yellow paint. Not a single piece of glass had broken, and no one was injured: I had been lucky. But when they returned and saw what had happened my mother and my father packed up the soil testing kit, and they put a lock on the basement cabinet. From my bed I could hear them arguing late into night about the danger I had put everyone in, and about whose fault that was.

*   *   *

"Come here, Ronnie," my junior high home room teacher crooned from the front of the room, "and please bring your notebook." Nobody ever called him Ronnie, but Ronald Liebman stood anyway and came forward. Mr. Pope opened the three-ring binder and studied the colored acetate dividers that Ronald had neatly labeled, and he gently removed each divider—Science, Math, French, Social Studies, English—and dropped it onto the floor. He unzipped the nylon pouch where Ronald had stored all his pens and pencils and slowly emptied that, too. The new, blue Bic ballpoints and the delicate mechanical pencil leads, stowed in their sleek, compact case; the clear arc of the retractor; the Tiny Tot stapler—each fell through the air before our eyes like a bewildered skydiver without a parachute, hitting the tile floor with a barely audible *ping* and skidding under someone's desk.

A few of us craned our necks gingerly over our desks for a view, but no one said a word or bent to retrieve any of Ronald Liebman's possessions lying in a heap of plastic and paper in the middle of the room. Mr. Pope had announced one day that each member of the class was exactly as important to him as a single pebble of sand on a beach. "Yes, pebble number two million seven hundred thousand forty-six?" he called out when Nancy Huang raised a hand to answer one of his questions. We understood Mr. Pope perfectly: we were small, details which the universe owed little notice.

We believed that we were forces of disorder—liable, on our own, to do damage; in need of restraint. One day in the lunch line a hulking, restless boy scooped a dish of jello from his tray and wildly flung it, leaving handfuls of scarlet cubes quivering on the walls like injured flesh. Since then the principal had made us march in single file to the cafeteria while he kept angry watch through his opened office door. Entering the long line that wound around the lunch room I would begin, instantly, to vibrate, barely able to hold my need in check. Mothers volunteering in hair nets and aprons drifted behind hot plates, holding up spatulas, prepared to dispense tuna melts. Angling for the biggest hunk of macaroni and cheese or the crusty corner piece of cherry cobbler, I anxiously counted my classmates ahead of me. At least once a week I would have to rummage through garbage for the retainer from my braces—uncanny pink plastic mold of my palate—because I'd stumbled in a daze to the open trash can after eating, and tipped my tray and its clammy jumble without a thought.

But in Mr. Pope's classroom we were relieved of the burden of chaos, and we complied with whatever forms of discipline he devised. He made Michael Weinstein, the class talker, squat silently in the corner. From my seat I could see Michael, low against the two walls, throughout the afternoon, as I prepared for the Illinois State Constitution test or made notes for my book report. If Michael made a sound of protest Mr. Pope would ask, without bothering to look up from his desk, "Is that the voice from the sewer?" Or he'd pronounce, "Fifteen more minutes, Weinstein!" Though many of us were Jewish, Mr. Pope informed the class that he had been a Nazi U-boat commander during World War II. There was deliberate cruelty in this, and I knew that my parents would want to be told. But I was too grateful for the fragile order that Mr. Pope brought to the day, and too captivated by the imagination with which he made our weaknesses interesting, to break the code of silence that each of us observed.

John Lubetsky squirmed all day at his desk, balling up wads of paper in his mouth and firing them through hollowed ballpoint pens at targets around the room. Mr. Pope made John sit in the wastebasket, where he struggled every few minutes to maneuver into a more bearable position, his butt perched on crumpled papers, his hands clenching the rim. Or Mr. Pope would raise the big window that opened from the high second story over the cement entryway to the school, and gesture to John with a curtly waved hand or a nod. John would climb out onto the ledge and Mr. Pope would close the window behind him and leave him hanging there with his legs dangling. "Where's John?" someone would remember, looking around, when the bell rang, and then Mr. Pope would return unhurriedly to the window and open it without speaking.

From the music room squeezed into the fourth floor attic we could hear boots slowly mounting the stairs one by one, as our teacher struggled to keep us focused on the story of Beethoven's sullen youthful rivalry with the graceful prodigy Mozart. Suddenly Tim Woolman burst through the classroom door and fell to his knees before us, clutching a long silk handkerchief to his heaving chest. Tim was wearing a pair of black knickers and a long cape that had obviously been taken from the prop closet backstage in the school auditorium. He waved the cape with a flourish as he gasped, "Oh, Mr. Gardenswarz! I tried to get to class on time! But spiders and scorpions were dropping from the ceiling and I had to fight my way here, step by step. I had to use my cape and my scarf to beat them off my face and my shoulders!" After letting a blank minute pass, our teacher rose from behind his long, scarred wooden desk and waved his conductor's baton weakly in Tim's direction, turning toward the measures of music chalked on the blackboard behind him and advising softly, "Well, OK, Tim. Very good. Just try not to let it happen again."

*   *   *

Our cooking class was laid out like a laboratory: long worktables around which tall swiveling stools were clustered. At the center of each table was a porcelain sink where we washed utensils after we'd finished preparing and serving our dishes. Whenever Miss Garrity, the cooking teacher, left the room we would spin at our places, pushing off from the worn wood, faster and faster, daring one another to the acid edge of nausea.

Miss Garrity demonstrated for us at her own model workstation, a white field of refrigerator and sink and stove, and burners lined with sparkling aluminum foil. Across the stovetop measuring devices were purposefully arrayed: bunched layers of stainless steel spoons poking out of a canister, and a fist-sized timer. We were forbidden to touch anything on Miss Garrity's counters. But through the glass oven door we could see the wire racks on which she baked wondrous fruit pies, criss-crossed with golden-browned strips of dough, and gravity-defying soufflés.

At the start of each class Miss Garrity would leave recipes for us in clipboards. For chicken à la king on toast points we were to begin by preheating our ovens and assembling the meat and the vegetables, then the flour and butter for thickening the cream sauce. We gently separated the spongy slices of Wonder Bread, removed the rough crust, and browned the pale triangles to fortify them against the sogging peas and the hard bits of carrots. We trimmed the slimy fat from chicken breasts and julienned the steamed flesh into cream of mushroom soup unloaded, in a jiggling lump, from a can.

Deep into darkening winter afternoons Miss Garrity would be flipping through her big notebook of breakfast ideas — pausing here and there, humming to herself, settling finally on a glossy illustration of broiled grapefruit sections topped with melted brown sugar, a dish that made so little sense to me that I concluded it must be meant for royalty. She propped up the recipe so that we could gather around and make up a list of ingredients together. Each of us used a paring knife to free the fruit's delicate membrane from the puffy, fragrant lining of the peel, and arranged the segments in a lightly buttered casserole dish. When the timer went off we consulted the instructions that we were required to keep in file folders and turned off our ovens, readying slotted spoons and rolls of foil. While we waited for the signal to open the oven doors, we thrust our hands into quilted mitts imprinted with dancing forks and knives or with smiling cupcakes, and beat them against each other like boxing gloves.

Miss Garrity regularly conducted spot inspections. When she blew her whistle we scattered fearfully to our assigned places. Counter by counter she would weave through the suddenly quieted room, indicating with a dark nod that a particular drawer or cabinet should be opened. Inside, we knew, all the silverware was to be precisely arranged and displayed: knives slotted neatly into racks; salad and dinner forks properly sorted into the shallow bins; mixing bowls nested in the correct sequence. The kitchen, Miss Garrity frequently reminded us, was the beating heart of household order. I was in awe of her expectation of perfection, which I knew I could never meet. When she found the cheap cap gun that my friend Lucy and I had slipped among the basting brushes, she fixed on us a look of pure revulsion.

After school we searched the telephone directory for Miss Garrity's home number and made phony calls to her from my mother and father's bedroom: "Is your refrigerator running? Then you'd better go catch it!" When I heard her voice at the other end of the line I imagined Miss Garrity at the command station of her personal kitchen, squeezing the phone to her ear with a dish-toweled shoulder as she eased a hot platter out of her oven. She would still be calling out with agitation—"Hello? Hello? *Hello?*"—as we banged down the receiver and dropped the phone onto the nightstand, bouncing giddily on my parents' big bed. Yet when Miss Garrity announced, at the end of eighth grade, that she was leaving Nichols Junior High School and getting married, I felt let down by the knowledge that an unknown man would be permitted to breach the boundaries of decorum that she had set for us, and that she would turn her attention on someone else.

*   *   *

"This is *precisely* what I told all of you <u>not</u> to do!" Mrs. Youngman called out—pointing a contemptuous finger at me and then twisting her whole body around at her desk to face the folding chairs that were arranged, in the manner of a fashion show, in a semi-circle around the rear of the room. I stopped just inside the doorway where I'd made my entrance and helplessly looked down, joining my classmates in reviewing my botched A-line skirt, my final sewing project. My mother and I had worked past midnight, but it still hung higher on the left than on the right. Even at a distance the fabric around the zipper must have looked irreparable, the visible result of countless despairing attempts into the night to heal the frayed parts into a whole. With a bent finger Mrs. Youngman signaled me: Approach. She reached down for the hem of my skirt, flipped it over on her lap as I stood with my eyes half shut, and invited everyone to leave their seats and examine the lurching line of stitches cutting a jagged border over my exposed knees. Beneath the long florescent lights I was locked in stunned quiet, dizzied by the freshly made skirts fanning out around me in an array of patterns and materials: madras, plaid, stripes, corduroy.

At the vast yard goods store where my mother and I shopped, bolts of cloth stood in long rows against the walls or were stacked lengthwise in massive piles. Their transformation into what Mrs. Youngman always referred to as "garments" managed at first to sparkle with hopefulness. I laid out the mysterious shapes of fabric beneath a McCall's or Butterick pattern and fixed them to the crackling tissue with a border of straight pins; I measured and cut each wobbling piece, painstakingly snipping out the tiny diamond guides that would serve as keys to fitting the puzzle together. But it was my own errors that would, in the end, be revealed. When I turned the final seam on my very first project, a square kerchief—white kittens dancing on a field of blue cotton—paws were jammed unforgivingly into tails and ears and whiskers.

One afternoon I steered the bucking needle through the tip of one of my fingers. Instantly the material began to soak up blood, leeching fraying streaks of fresh red into the weave of the fabric. Mrs. Youngman waved me out of the room with a disgusted sigh—"Just go to the nurse's office"—and I set off alone down the hall, a tunnel of subdued light punctuated by the glowing windows set into each massive classroom door. I already knew that Miss Lee, the junior high school nurse, would admit me reluctantly—complaining that I had arrived without a teacher's signed pass, insisting that I must have been careless with the sewing machine—and bandage my finger roughly without even waiting for the bleeding to stop.

Each year Miss Lee tested our eyesight. I waited my turn in the dark, glasses folded safely in my hand. One by one the other members of my class picked out letters from the spreading pool of light on the wall and called them out loudly until she was satisfied. And every year Miss Lee would treat my claim that I couldn't make out a single letter as an act of insubordination. "Squint!" she would order, and even though I drew in the muscles around my eyes to see what all my classmates saw—E-A-P-R; big block letters crowding the very top row—every line still leaked sharpness at the edges.

On other days I would creep to Miss Lee's threshold, whispering *cramps*. While the pain was rising in my belly at my homeroom desk I imagined myself as a slumped figure in a cartoon panel, surrounded by vibrating lines. In front of me Eddie Steinberg filled the ridged pencil tray on his desktop from the class watering can and sailed his pencils back and forth. Every so often he would raise the tray and dump the water on Ethan Berman in the seat ahead of him, making it look for the rest of the day as though Ethan had wet his pants. I suspected that my own underwear bore blood-red stains, and I could not risk making myself the object of similar humiliation.

In her office Miss Lee would quiz me, searching my face for evidence of insincerity. When she was satisfied, she would usher me onto one of the cots that she'd set up in her back room. There she had carved out for freshly adolescent girls a place where embarrassment and shame could be tended like a secret garden. A tall screen and a heavy door separated us from the daily business of the nurse's office that was carried out in the open, from the vision and hearing tests and the requests for bandaids and ice packs. If a custodian or a technician had to pass by on his way to perform a repair, Miss Lee would cry out, "Man!" Otherwise she would tell me to pull my knees to my chest and go back to her work. An entire afternoon could pass while I waited there, curled and aching, watching the light slowly change through the high corner windows and listening for familiar voices beyond the closed door.

*   *   *

Our school finished each term with a one-thousand-yard run. Our path was a beaten, long loop inside the chain link fence that surrounded the school playing fields. The sun jabbed the metal netting and flared at our eyes as we passed the front gate and then made an even longer turn around the block.

Far ahead of me I could see legs churning rhythmically forward, and the leader drawing the rest around turns like an engine pulling a train. But no matter how hard I hoped it would be different this year, I would go breathless by the time I first circled the field and pounded out onto the sidewalk in my gymsuit. A snap or two would always come undone at my chest or near my hips, and I would be exposed in public at midday. Sometimes—the worst times—a passing car would slow and coast along with me as I straggled farther and farther behind. I could see the driver laughing or a hand saluting ironically from the passenger seat as the car pulled away. When he saw me stumble back onto the field, hardly moving at all anymore, my gym teacher would run the last paces alongside me, mocking my fatigue.

As I finally turned away, I could see just beyond the baseball diamond my classmate Peter Deutsch. Oblivious to the figures hunched in sweaty uniforms on the grass taking long gulps of air after their runs, Peter would be swinging placidly from a tree in his street clothes.

Peter Deutsch was a mystery to me. He was as tall as most of our teachers, and he dressed like an adult: in cuffed khaki pants, blue button-down collar work shirts, and brown leather shoes. When the principal delivered him to our class for the first time, it was already the middle of the school year. Peter waved hello when he heard his name and allowed himself to be jammed into a desk without a word.

He seemed even more inept than I, so I made Peter my project. At first he didn't talk at all, only smiling and shaking or nodding his head whenever someone addressed him or asked

~66~

him to read or write. I sat beside him in class, gently repeating key concepts in social science—gross national product; port city; crop rotation; separation of powers—and indicating with exaggerated hand motions that he should write his name and today's date in the upper right hand corner of every homework sheet. He smiled and nodded his head. But when he took up his pen it was to cover each page with crude drawings of what looked like jungle animals among stands of canopied trees. I explained to Mr. Gardenswarz that Peter would never be able to summarize the plot of *Madame Butterfly*, and I discretely asked our French teacher Mademoiselle Dorin if Peter could be excused from diagramming the parts of sentences and from conjugating French verbs. He didn't even speak English, really!

One afternoon Peter silently waved me over to his desk. And into my ear he said, quite distinctly, "Never mind: I'll be moving to Africa soon." After class Peter revealed to me his plan. He was fifteen years old and just biding his time in junior high school until he could drop out at age sixteen. He showed me a little spiral notebook in which he was recording the Tarzan language he picked up from movies and comic strips, and practiced alone in preparation for his new life.

I nodded without a word, stunned by the confidence with which Peter described his half-baked scheme and, even more, by his emptiness of interest in what anyone else thought of him. I could not imagine either that ease or that freedom. I was forever scanning around myself, braced for humiliation.

On Saturday nights at the Women's Club of Evanston, where my parents had enrolled me in social dancing lessons, I was always the one struggling with my pantyhose in the power room when the call came to join the line in the long, chandeliered foyer. All the boys and girls would be matched up, two by two, for their dramatic entrance into the ballroom, where they parted into ragged waves that deposited them on opposite sides of the room. Mr. and Mrs. Walther, our instructors, would glide in, arm in arm like a movie couple, to demonstrate each dance in the spotlit center of the room. She wore an unlikely yellow skirt that retained an element of the provocative even in a solemn two-step; he a string tie and heavily styled hair, at once Gene Autry and Maurice Chevalier. They smiled unceasingly at one another. Then they each took a bow, signaling that the boys should cross over to the girls' side of the room and select partners.

Around me every couple seemed to be moving in rhythmic unison to the back-and-forth beats of a *cha-cha* record while I clawed the shoulders of Paul Klein's shiny sport jacket. My parents had joined forces with Paul's to pressure the class's public school sponsors into admitting Jews for the first time to the Women's Club, and week after week I despaired of what they witnessed from the ballroom balcony. I wondered what my mother and my father saw as they watched their daughter, waiting always for Paul in the stiff party dress that she'd settled for at the end of an anxious stream of visits to plus-size shops in the city—waiting to be chosen, dying to disappear.

*   *   *

I wake, in the still heat of summer darkness, to the dusty smell of canvas. Or am I awake? Still a sleepwalker at home in adolescence I am afraid for myself, reluctant to give in to slumber. In the night at Girl Scout camp I might easily become lost— vanished in the forest like a child in a fairy tale.

I feel nervously for the flashlight that I keep with my folded glasses next to one of the legs of my cot. My mother has marked my name on it in block letters, in permanent black magic marker. The only one in our tent who can't sleep through the night, I tiptoe out the flap door of the tent, anxious not to make a sound, aimed toward the opening of the path through the woods.

In a clearing ahead is a wooden building stained the color of cedar. Beneath the droning bug lights the walls glow an unnatural shade of yellow; when I step close my shadow tips across the jaundiced, flattened dirt. Inside, an enormous basin rises like an altar out of the concrete floor. At bedtime all the campers in my unit brush their teeth and wash their faces here, giggling in the cold, ringing evening air in pajamas and wool socks and slippers. But now the whole structure hovers softly like an alien space station, spotlighted within a blackly huddling ring of blurred trees. My loneliness can no longer be put off. Shivering in the flip-flops that my mother insisted I wear in any public shower—the flimsy pink soles gritty with dirt and pine needles from the forest floor—I let myself cry in the damp dark, the dew rising around me at the far brink of dawn.

For our pantomime this last night of camp I played Winnie the Pooh: pausing after a hearty lunch at the entrance to Piglet's tree trunk house, rubbing my stomach with satisfaction and contemplating my exit with a cocked hand. I took a last hopeful look behind me at the honey jar, rising to my toes to search over the rim, turning to step up into the doorway. And as I pushed off on my right foot I imagined my body catching against wood as it poured into the opening, filling the space, tightly wedging into it—completely stuck.

I closed my eyes and felt my legs batting uselessly behind me, my hands clutching at rough, crumbling bark, flailing for a hold from which I could unlock my honey-swollen middle and drag my dangling weight out onto the forest floor. I could hear anticipatory laughter start to break out as soon as I began to twist my caught hips, even before I cupped my hand to my mouth and lip-synched, "Halloo, Piglet!"—and I suddenly wanted someone to rush onstage to help me. Piglet would soon begin pulling at my feet, crying out that he was trapped, for his little house had no back door. And I couldn't save him, or myself, and everyone could see.

Hunger Artist

For Ellen Wertheim and Richard McCann

"Isn't it love we're sent here for?"
—Bonnie Raitt, "You"

With my cousin Jerome's wedding coming up my mother drives me to Chicago's Devon Avenue, where the shops owned by elderly Jewish Eastern European immigrants cater to "special" sizes. "I don't suppose you'd have a strapless bra for her," she sighs, glancing doubtfully back and forth between my bulging T-shirt and the stocky matrons positioned with folded arms in front of the racks. Among our own, my mother can share her descending mood of resignation. At one of the stores where we're regulars she hauls skirts and blouses back to the dressing room where I wait unenthusiastically. In her trim cotton camp shirt and A-line skirt my mother takes stock, trying to keep an open mind as I try on each item. But I know it's useless to imagine that I will like anything here, or that anything the store carries will actually be in fashion; it is enough that we find clothes that fit. This is my punishment for giving in to hunger: exile from the land of proud bodies, bodies that lilt through space in bright, form-fitting cloth.

In the jammed, stuffy corridor at the rear of the store I bang blindly into hanging dresses and coats, and middle-aged ladies with mouths full of pins stand back from their handiwork crowing unlikely promises: "When it's hemmed, you'll look so cute, doll!" Silently I adjust the limbs that they finger and point, lifting and dropping my arms so that the saleswomen can slide on sleeves; lowering my eyes as they roughly unbutton a shirt and leave me standing in my underwear while they search out a bigger size for me, their acquiescent manikin. Every so often the owner will steer me into the harsh light of the front window to model something for her cashier husband, the only person more out of place in the store than I am. He nods a clipped OK, while I feel myself fill up with shame as viscous and tight as oil topping off a drum.

I sulk in the car on the way home, closing my eyes and erasing my mother on the seat beside me, the sticky summer streets and the interminable stoplights that slow our escape. Around me gravity gathers force: my immobilizing, despairing fate. What would it feel like to break free, to let go of heaviness? I read compulsively about the astronauts, the only humans who have broken through that barrier. "The best part of being in space is being weightless," one writes, and I thrill with the possibility. In *Life* magazine, photographs show astronauts playfully squirting orange juice and releasing peanuts to float free, out of gravity's greedy reach. Circling in their spacecraft, they drift up to the ceiling to feed out of vacuum-packed envelopes that they penetrate with straws—chocolate milk and macaroni-and-cheese that they reconstitute from powder by adding water from their storehouses on board—and turn unhurried somersaults over one another. In T-shirts and boxer shorts they hover above the instrument panels in the command capsule, bouncing gently from wall to wall. In Chicago's Museum of Science and Industry gift shop I buy foil packets of the ice cream that they supposedly eat and imagine them touching the dry blocks with their tongues, waiting for the stuff to come back to life as they stare through the night at the suspended, luminous marble of Planet Earth.

Thanks to the astronauts we too can see ourselves new from outer space, our whirling planet tracked in breathtaking, impossible laps. In the miraculous images that NASA beams down, the sprawling coast of New England comes into view whole; we can see entire continents, long, creeping rivers, the Alps. The puzzle of our world is completed—the Dead Sea set neatly into its little spot in a glowing puddle of desert, a perfect fit. The astronauts are perfect, too, speeding unerringly home through the flaming atmosphere. We can see on TV each smoky capsule bobbing in the midst of ocean, the door flung open, the relieved faces emerging through the capsule's pierced skin, the lips forming victorious smiles.

And yet even they must have their private moments, the times when bodies make their graceless, earthly needs felt, when the camera is turned off and the screens in living rooms across our globe go dark. I wonder if astronauts struggle with their soiled clothes in the dizzy waking hour that passes for dawn in an orbiting space capsule. Some nights they must shiver in the airless silence, knowing that they could be cut off forever from the only life they know, spinning away at the other end of a telescope.

*   *   *

"Do you *have* to eat that?" my Aunt Ida demands at the end of dinner, when everyone is lingering over a pot of smoky tea and a long platter of brownies and mandelbrot. "Yes," I snap. "Yes, I *do* have to." And I eat half a brownie without giving anyone eye contact. My body's accumulating bulk has evolved among my relatives into an approved topic of conversation. My mother makes little effort to lower her voice at the other end of the table, where she sits with her sisters. "I don't keep any sweets or chips in the house any more. I can't figure out what she's eating!" No one turns back to me for an answer.

I bide my time, listening to them and not listening, drifting from the table with its dusting of nutshells and crumbs, the half-empty teacups and the saucers dotted with cherry pits. We'll be going home soon, in any case. Soon I will be promising my mother that I've brushed my teeth, and closing the bedroom door and stretching out on my bedspread. Underneath my pillow the package of M&M's that I secretly bought and set aside is waiting, meticulously hoarded. I could easily finish off the whole in two quick handfuls, but I never do. Before I eat a single one, I sort them by color, separating the piles along the top of the sheet. I debate first between the dark brown and the light brown candies, my two favorites. Then the red ones, followed by the greens; and the yellows and the oranges that I leave, always, for last. I hold them in my mouth in groups of either three or four and delicately let each shell dissolve and expose the soft center; I turn over the velvet milk chocolate disks with my tongue and feel them melt together into a single luxurious mass. Or I gently crack smooth pink and white Good-and-Plenty pellets—licking and sucking the fleshy licorice inside to which sharp bits of candy are stuck like the shells of hard-boiled eggs. Once I'm finished I hide the empty package in my desk, ramming it into a deepening mound.

My mother piles peas and broccoli on our plates beside lamb chops still sizzling from the broiler; chicken parts crusted with barbecue sauce; celery sticks marinated in bottled Italian dressing. But my favorite meals fly solo: tuna pot pies stacked in snug boxes in the freezer compartment; six-inch pizzas shrink-wrapped in cellophane jackets, trailing shreds of mozzarella cheese that cling to the clear plastic. I unload the steamy pie crusts from the oven and eat by myself in front of forbidden TV spy shows, *The Man from U.N.C.L.E.* or *The Avengers.* On summer afternoons when my parents are at work I crank open cans of Campbell's soup and eat the salty broth — the ragged chunks of beef and the cubes of carrot and potato — in old pie tins, sitting on the back steps, imagining myself a famished Civil War soldier, legitimately carnal. Sometimes I add leftovers from the refrigerator to the mix, picking up bones with my bare hands and gnawing at the cold flesh.

My younger sister dawdles at the refrigerator, opening and closing it, casually scraping Tupperware over the wire shelves inside, ignoring my mother's tired complaining: "Are you planning to pay this month's electric bill out of your allowance?" Anita takes her time, not the slightest bit afraid of threats, casually knocking a ketchup bottle with her elbow as she pries open a jar of peach halves, bouncing the laden door with her hip each time it starts to swing shut. Steam rolls over the cold metal as she tastes things: tuna salad sticky with mayonnaise and pickle relish, heaped in a plastic container; bologna and cream cheese rolls, pierced with colored plastic toothpicks and stacked in neat rows in a tin foil tent. Or she might just reach in with sudden decisiveness, replace a lid with a snap, and let the door fall behind her as she leaves the room.

But I am hostage to mysterious forces. My secret domain is the basement freezer, where food is preserved in its most radical form; isolated from the crude momentum of hunger expecting to be satisfied, the dull routines of daily feeding. Only a narrow shaft of natural light pokes weakly into the cavernous laundry room. And when I pull on one of the long strings that hang from naked bulbs down there, a hazy yellow cone takes shape around me, cutting me off from the world above. Inside the freezer everything has been wrapped tight, sealed with masking tape in the flat gray boxes in which my father's shirts come home from the cleaner.

Barricaded in there is my mother's most extravagant work: miniature cheesecakes, left over from my bat mitzvah, complete down to the last detail—the graham cracker crust, the filling, the glazed fruit topping. My mother bought special pans to make them, so small that only two strawberry halves or three or four blueberries fit on top of each one. Her methodically layered toffee bars—crust, candy, milk chocolate, slivered almonds—are stacked as trimly as a brick wall.

I carefully peel back the chilled, stiff tape. I painstakingly rearrange the contents of each box, attempting to erase my intrusion by creating new patterns of circles and squares, a little more shallow and sparse every time. And then I give in, leaning, intoxicated, against one of the clammy basement walls. The little cheesecakes fill my mouth entirely, soft crumb and icy cream melting against the tender lining of my cheeks, still cold, slipping into my throat. I take each toffee bar apart with my tongue and my teeth and warm it, saving the tiny slab of hard candy to suck slowly or to bite into small shards. "This is the last time, I promise," I'll plead later—and believe myself—after my mother discovers the pathetic leavings of her raided storehouse, revealed at the last minute as inadequate for a dinner party.

*　　　　　　*　　　　　　*

Uncle Bob and Aunt Myrtle were childless and eager to spoil. At every meal their table was heaped with slices of turkey and with brazen, rare roast beef cleaved as thin as red tissue; with coleslaw and potato salad as creamy as a dessert. Nearby, on a Naugahyde couch, Uncle Bob laid out his enormous body, the distended flesh of an aging trucker, and watched through half-shut, dreamy eyes as his wife unloaded their cargo of excess.

It was forever a party there, at which we were the featured guests, feted with treats and surprises, entertained by appliances. The ordered *whizz* of traffic receded behind us, behind the narrow cement curb warming in the late sun next to my parents' parked car. Inside, in those humming, air conditioned rooms, the refrigerator and cabinets were stocked with rich inventory: chocolate chip cookies and Good Humor bars; bags of cheese twists that we were free to open without permission from our parents. Aunt Myrtle brought home delicacies from the Marshall Field's gourmet department and let us feed the cardboard containers into her trash compactor. We stood back, behind her outstretched arm, listening to the ominous surge until, to our delight, a set of anonymous cubes popped magically out. Even their toaster—a lavish stainless steel contraption that produced eight slices at a time—was nothing like our own workmanlike little machine. It would be a battle, when evening came, to pry my sister and me away from the only color television set we'd ever seen—and a letdown to face Ed Sullivan and *Bonanza* at our house the following Sunday, when they were drained to black and white.

My aunt and uncle's miniature Doberman Pinscher, Caesar, a caricature of a dog, bounced and barked when we arrived, his brittle nails clicking hysterically on the linoleum. Every December we received in the mail a new calendar headed by a formal portrait of Caesar—often in a bow tie or a swanky turtleneck—that my mother put away with the Christmas gifts sent by our gentile neighbors. A framed enlargement of Caesar was propped up on the wet bar where my cousin Glenn and I played bartender before dinner. The two of us flipped the oversized nickel faucets on and off and ceremoniously prepared drinks for everyone, setting out glasses on lime green cocktail napkins printed with black bubbles. My mother once told me that Uncle Bob and Aunt Myrtle had longed for a child of their own but had been frightened off from adoption by neigh-borhood rumors of white families who had been tricked into accepting black babies. Even I sensed a charge let loose around them, floundering in the air like free ions; lonesomeness and need as palpable as my aunt and uncle's generosity.

And indeed I knew that there was something secret from us in that house, a dark, untouched heart. For upstairs lay a silent parallel universe: the life to which Aunt Myrtle and Uncle Bob returned by themselves when we had gone. There was a second kitchen, identical in shape to the one below; and a second dining room just over the one where they fed their guests. A set of Corningware baking dishes was nested on the immaculate counter. A spotless mixing spoon rested on a sky blue Delft tile. On the shelves of an enormous breakfront a collection of china statuettes was set out on display: pink ballerinas on fragile tiptoes; an intricate carrousel ringed with multicolored horses carrying ladies in plumed hats and a pair of lovers squeezed into a single glossy saddle; a frozen grouping of poodles and collies and sour-faced King Charles spaniels. The upstairs living room was lined with heavy sofas whose upholstery lay hidden beneath a milky layer of plastic slipcovers, though no dirt or disorder seemed likely to penetrate the vacuum up there.

I wondered what Aunt Myrtle and Uncle Bob said to one another when they climbed the narrow, aluminum-tipped stairs to their upstairs apartment after our noisy departure; when they reached the landing where the wall-to-wall carpet began its lush spread. Did they ever bend together over their glass cases, admiring a new figurine? Did they sometimes surprise one another by filling up one of the bowls in the kitchen with a midnight snack? Through Uncle Bob and Aunt Myrtle's bedroom door a stiff satin canopy glinted, but I couldn't imagine them reaching for one another in the dusky hush. I never saw them even hold hands in the loud rooms downstairs where they fed and tended to us.

*   *   *

What secrecy love hoards! In the closeness of the womb Siamese twins embrace, heart to heart, in their tandem float, during the long wait for the journey to the surface. Some—most closely, most dangerously entwined—may even share with one another a single beating heart, a heart that pumps warm blood from one body to another, night and day and forever. Only the two of them know the hidden route through which love passes in the darkness, the fragile cord that binds them, and the tremulous hunger that cannot count on being reached. Their fate in the daylight is already sealed: a surgeon will mark a black X on a blackboard outline of the doomed twin, the child for whom there is not enough heart for two—not enough for both life and love.

*   *   *

"Am I pretty?" I used to ask my mother. "What a question!" she always exclaimed, immediately closing the subject: "You don't need to be pretty!" Was that my mother's secret, the secret of her contentment? Not to ask for too much, not to be hungry for what she knew she couldn't have?

On holidays, uncles and aunts and cousins crowded the small rooms of my grandparents' house. My mother and her sisters always came early to lengthen the table with heavy, notched leaves and to add pads and tablecloths, to squeeze folding chairs in between the overworked pieces of the formal dining room set that my grandmother and grandfather had stubbornly saved for during the Depression. The three women labored together quietly, polishing the prized silver and setting out the dinner plates and salad plates and soup bowls, the massive serving dishes and the flower arrangements. "You need to help, too," my mother would urge me as I watched my cousin Cary flirt with her medical student boyfriend. Cary worked a couple of fingers slowly through her hair, following the long, straight strands down from her perfect part, feeling expertly for split ends, while I thought with despair about my own tangle of cowlicks. Soon the meal would begin, and the hours of serving and clearing food, of cleaning up after massive eating. My aunts would take chicken parts in their hands, breaking the little bones of the wings and the vertebra of the back and the neck and sucking out the marrow, leaving heaps of chewed flesh and cartilage on their dinner plates.

When the three sisters finished their preparations, each of them would take off her apron and go to change clothes and put on her earrings and her makeup in the tiny back bedroom where one of them had always slept when they were children. It was there, in that back bedroom, in decades-ago childhood, that they had gone with their bachelor uncle. A tailor recently immigrated from Poland, he came on Sunday afternoons to share some company and a home-cooked meal, and to help out by altering the children's hand-me-down clothes. He would take my mother in her turn and draw the drapes for her fittings. He watched my mother undress and he placed his hands on her, lightly at the start, measuring and calculating and fingering the old smocks and blouses, estimating the life left in the fabric. And then, as her eyes wandered to the stained wallpaper with its red and green roosters and pecking hens, he hungrily felt the swelling of her hips and breasts—those newnesses, hardly familiar yet to her, maybe even recognized for the first time under his attentive fingers. When the bedroom door finally opened my mother would have dressed again in her own clothes, put on her shoes. She would return to her sisters and her mother and the dining room table without a word about what had happened to her in the afternoon shadows, and pick at the brisket and the roasted potatoes that lay in congealing fat on her plate.

"Be careful not to hug your sons too much," my grandmother would warn many years later, when her oldest daughter became a mother. "And don't you kiss your boys." Waiting in her darkening living room for dusk and the lighting of the candles, my grandmother stood watch near the heavy table where we gathered before Shabbat dinner. Already my aunt's fate was festering within her. Organ to organ—kidney to lung to brain— over ten long years the cancer would spread in secret until it was too late for even the savagery of surgeons' knives to reach and to cut. Irrepressible in her youth, my aunt had roosted on the cement stoop after school, waiting to leap down the three steps to kick passing strangers in the shins and run off, laughing, down the sidewalk. But in the end her three boys and my mother and my mother's daughters would sponge her exhausted, wounded body while she turned hot, beseeching eyes on us. We couldn't reach her pain and we were already becoming strangers to her. Though I loved her and I had told her so, many times, I knew that she could no longer hear me and I knew that she had stopped caring that I was there. As she clawed the sheets, her starved hips showed, shrunken, through the twisted gown.

*   *   *

Like an animal I am always on the lookout, aware of the scarce resources of survival. "You are not actually a member of our family," I tell my sister when she is four or five years old, "We found you rolling in the dust on a lonely Texas road, and brought you back to Chicago with us in the car." She sparkles just the same—fearless, a sprite. I nudge her out the attic window in our new house and close it behind her, leaving her out on the roof until her astonished, beating fists start to leave marks on the glass that I think I might be called on to explain. I stuff her headfirst into the dryer and turn it on. Upside down her T-shirt slips up her chest and reveals skin so like mine that I feel afraid for myself, and I yank open the door, already heating up, and scoop her out.

In my head a decade later I write away the members of my family in a tragic car accident, so that I can be adopted by my Girl Scout camp counselors and their boyfriends. They devote their complete attention to me, their only child. We all live together in a sunny, open-plan modern house not far from my deceased parents' aging warren of unfinished rooms. We take relaxing vacations in Florida, where I read paperbacks on the beach in a bright red bikini, tanning my lean body. My secret life is completely known to me, down to the last eager detail: we drive a yellow Chevrolet Impala convertible and a brown Porsche; each of us has our own brand new Raleigh ten-speed; we own Clue and Risk and an ebony chess set, and we leave the game boards on the dining room table and just eat around them until we're finished playing. We keep dishes of candy on the grand piano and the sleek glass coffee table in the living room, and all of us help ourselves to Coffee Nips and Hershey's Kisses whenever we want to, casually dropping the bunched, shiny wrappers into the trash. One of my fantasy guardians always has time to help me with my homework and to tuck me into bed at night.

Keened to the presence of competitors I have become an expert in hunger—prepared to wield hunger to hurt, to let need linger cruelly into starvation. Back at my parents' house, neighbors leave their canary with me while they winter in Florida. His name is Pretty Bird, and in fact he seems at first like something bright and sonorous, a treat, a talented visitor who might perform for us if we are good. When Mrs. Barry brings him over, his cage is draped with a felt blanket that she lifts slowly like a stage curtain. In his elaborately bronzed cage are wooden perches layered like parallel bars and a bell that he jingles throughout the long day, calling for food and attention, until I drag him down to the basement. In a quiet moment between sets of ping pong my friends and I might hear him— whistling, more and more briefly; shuffling in the sandpaper, stuck with droppings, along the dry, husky floor of his cage. But mostly I push him deeper into the shadows, where the noise of the washing machine and the dryer drown him out. I stop remembering to keep his plastic troughs filled with seed mix and his dish filled with water, and no one notices when he stops singing, or even when I secretly collect his little body in a Kleenex and dump it onto the compost heap in our backyard, just barely sorry.

THE INVISIBLE WORLD

I

Alone at night I cannot keep from filling my bedroom with fear. I sweat under the covers, ashamed of the wiry surge of terror building in my throat. I sense the lush stands of elms and lindens that line our long block reaching toward one another to blot out the moonlight, I can feel blackness tightening around me. Below the landing where I creep in my pajamas, steps drop off into nothingness, and I know that the stuff of my nightmares lies in wait in the shadows where the staircase turns; where the approach of Nazis and savage birds of prey will be muffled by the pile carpeting. I know that I will bolt before the night lifts, across the lightless hall to my parents, and that my mother and my father will have no patience with me when I burst one more time through their shut door in tears and I fall on them in their bed.

The pounding pulse of the universe seems too close, all around me, during those long, dark nights. The familiar details of my room—the whistling stir of the hamster's exercise wheel, the reek of urine-soaked cedar shavings, the smooth perfection of the new bookshelf that my father and I lovingly sanded together—evaporate as I return, helplessly, to the same waking nightmare. Behind my clenched eyelids, two shadows expand at cartoon speed—collide—instantly shrink to a single concentrated dot—and, in the next split second, vanish. Light and darkness, sperm and egg: each time, blunt forces gather, find one another, and take unexpected forms, renewing my shivering uncertainty. With just the slightest jiggle, everything could shift: I could live in a different house, with a different family and a different name; I would have different parents. In the morning I go down to the basement, shaky and doubtful, and confront my mother at the ironing board: "I will stay with you, whoever you are," I promise, as her laughter turns to bewilderment, "but you have to take off the mask and tell me what you've done with my father and mother."

At Lee Street beach I drift off from my mother and my sister to explore one of the aging piers that bracket the shore. In winter, snow blows across the sand and buries the pier; bitter spray coats every surface in slick layers, and the nearest shallow water steadily freezes, closing in on the columns like arctic pack ice. Now, in summer, the cement shows the wear of cold and heat and the constant press of damp. Through widening cracks in the massive blocks of gravely amalgam I can see rough water swirling, and rusted iron rods poking savagely through the reinforced concrete. As I pick my way along the choppy pier I pass the line of orange safety buoys that the strongest swimmers shadow, and I move out it seems onto the lake itself, vast and blank. Suddenly, with my back to the beach, the lapping waves feel of less certain origin, a force drawing me out dangerously to the far horizon. I shiver and turn, at the limit of my nerve.

Another beach day, when the sun has exhausted us, my sister and I return home to find the back door ajar. At once I can feel suspicion rise in me, like acid; my fearsome knowledge of the presence of strangers. Still in my sand-stuck bathing suit, I make a series of lone forays into the house, collecting every sharp object that might be used against us: steak knives, carving knives, barbecue skewers. In the climbing heat I remember the fireplace equipment, the viciously pronged log iron and the heavy shovel, meant for ashes but in the wrong hands, potentially, a weapon. And the corncob holders, green and yellow plastic knobs that I add to the clatter of metal piled in the backyard.

By the time my mother backs into the garage and begins unloading groceries, my work is complete. It will take her weeks to recover what I have buried: the invisible blades bunched in the dirt around her ant-encrusted peonies, around her tulips; in the matted, low lilies of the valley.

II

My parents brought home to their children miraculous kits in which the speeding world was broken down into compliant components, waiting to be assembled. Our family built whole machines out of the scrambled fragments that we unpacked from cardboard boxes: cockpit and chassis in functioning detail, down to the hand painted headlights and the fiery decals that we applied, last, along the wing of a scale model World War II fighter jet or the hood of a plastic Corvette. A richness of new products lined the supermarket aisles: freeze-dried soups, frozen TV dinners, miracles of time-saving meals, gimmicky cereals. In a cellophane envelope hidden like a charm in the Cocoa Krispies I was rewarded with the pieces of an intricate rickshaw that I put together all by myself and ran for weeks on a string line along the kitchen table.

For my tenth birthday my parents gave me the boxed Visible Woman. I sorted her reproductive system into the palm of my own hand, turning the uterus and the ovaries against one another like marbles. Before she could be brought to life over two hundred separate anatomical parts had to be detached, one by one, from plastic stalks. Around the dully colored core of spine and brain I eased into place the two kidneys, capped by adrenal glands. And the byzantine skeletal system: the ribs winding around the lungs; the stream of bones narrowing from the pelvis to the feet; the delicate strings of wrist and finger links suspended from each arm. I had to jam the heart, with its awkward aorta, into the crowded chest cavity, just above the bulging stomach. When I snapped the clear windshield of skin over the whole Woman, her breasts and hips swelled transparently on the display stand, suddenly betraying her nakedness.

My mother ordered from Kimberly Clark a large, plain carton supplied with a cheerfully illustrated pamphlet and an assortment of Kotex sanitary napkins, arranged in ascending order of absorbency. She couldn't know that late one night, at a slumber party, Georgeanne Moore had already revealed how once a month each of us would be having a baby that would pop and bleed on its way out. I could feel my mother's plump body shifting on my narrow twin bed as she opened the box, trying to come close, and I could hardly imagine what to do with my own apprehensive, unready body. I anxiously picked open the hospital-white bundles from the box and uncurled them and set them out, like fresh doll mattresses, on my bed. The rough stuffing seemed as flimsy as my mother's unlikely promise: Because you know, you will never have to be ashamed, as we were.

Below the surface of the visible, knowledge remained to me, like the body, mysterious, clandestine, full with emotion. I never revealed to my parents the days I passed in the grammar school nurse's office, deep in the basement below my fifth-grade classroom. For me alone Miss Wertheim would crack a thermometer on her desk to free the mercury; and I would chase the escaping silver as it shivered into the channels between floor tiles or lurched out her office door. Sometimes Miss Wertheim and I would dismantle the contents of her lunch. I had never seen or touched a whole green pepper before she brought one out of her paper sack, and I remember the jolt I felt when she first bit into it, like an apple, and her soft laugh when she saw my startled look. Bent close over the deep green globes, the two of us would trace the surface of each pepper with our fingers, following the crevices and curves as they dipped and rose. We pierced the tight skin with the kitchen knife that she kept next to the erasers in her drawer, and shook the seeds over the lunch bag that we had scissored open and spread out over the report forms she left scattered on her desk.

III

Who would make good on science's promise to yield revelation; to compel the world to come close and unmask itself? The bomb was no longer new, Oppenheimer and Einstein had already apologized, and still the atom remained a mystery: invisible, pulsing reservoir of chaos. In the eighth grade I wrote to Edward Teller, a man with few regrets, for an explanation of nuclear fission. Teller mailed me a 5x7 publicity photo of himself, and I let my science teacher, Mr. Barton, slip the manila envelope into the top drawer of his steel gray desk.

Everyone laughed at Stephen Gardner when he told the class that he'd washed his plenaria colony down the drain the night before he finished his independent project. In front of an empty fishbowl Stephen sadly unfolded the long stream of graph paper on which he had recorded the daily progress of his experiment. Following his presentation I gave my own indifferent salamander a vicious pinch so that it would rear up on its hind legs, a frightened dinosaur in the palm of my hand. Sometimes during the next class period we would slip down our shirtsleeves the chicken legs that we had dissected, so that when we raised our arms to answer a question we could pull on the tendons and make the scaly claws open and close.

And yet we were invited to lay the same mocking hands on the carcasses of living things, to spill the leavings of life onto old newspapers. I had heard that Mr. Barton was an Eskimo, and that his tribal totem was among the strange carved poles that we gaped at along Lake Shore Drive on the way home from my grandparents' house. A peculiar current charged the room as he unpacked a big, official-looking box and handed out cows' eyes in oozing sacs of formaldehyde. I could hardly look at the chunky white globes, swollen with red and blue threads, as they swung slowly from side to side in their plastic bags, sealed casually, like sandwiches, with wire twists. Old enough to realize that we had come suddenly into a new potency, we were yet too young to sense in ourselves the flirtatious shadow of cruelty, the power to ruin; or to guess that our every act could leave a scar.

All along the big table each of us released a load of slime and chemicals, unsheathed a scalpel, and tapped the delicate membrane coating each eye. Near me I could see Tim Woolman taking a slower look at the eyeball rocking unevenly on the butcher paper in front of him. Mr. Barton's voice drifted into the background as Tim quietly picked up his scalpel and began with the tip to trace his own route on the surface of the eye: around the black ring of the iris and the dark, empty pupil at the center. With a surgeon's confidence he sliced into the flesh. Tim took in his fingers the lens of the cow's eye—as plain an object as a discarded piece of costume jewelry—and dropped it into his mouth, and swallowed.

No one saw but me. Something opened, then closed, like a secret. For just one terrible moment I had stumbled near to the trembling body of order, and I saw that the world was as small as we were, that it could come apart at our touch.

IV

My father's father was born in this country, but he never seemed at ease anywhere. He was forever pointing his household upward, uprooting his wife to keep pace with Chicago's rising skyline. First it was to the top floor of the newest building in their own South Side neighborhood, near where they had raised their children. But before long he was turning my reluctant grandmother toward the other side of the city, where they knew no one, to the twenty-fourth floor of a just-completed highrise. At his window above the northern lakeshore my grandfather spent long, unspeaking hours keeping anxious watch over the construction site across the street, until the steel frame rose to meet his eye. And in his late seventies he rented yet another apartment, ten stories higher.

The oil firm that my grandfather worked for, as an accountant, seemed to share his craziness for the sky. Their offices were for many years in the forty-four-story Prudential Building, then Chicago's highest; and when the stark, black-crossed John Hancock was completed—in its turn the tallest building in the world—they were among the first tenants. I would sometimes skip my high school classes and take the train to visit my grandfather at whatever high place he was working. Already drunk by noon, he would struggle to focus on my face while he ran his fingers absently through my hair and called me his *shaineh maideleh*; his pretty little girl. Higher yet on the building's observation deck, we would gaze together at the city spread below; and I wondered on overcast days if for once we saw the same indistinct world, unsteady and blurred, through the passing clouds.

After my parents' divorce we traveled together: my father's parents, my sister and I, my father and his new girlfriend Sharon. While my sister nested between my grandparents' soft laps in the back seat, I fit myself between Sharon and the closed car door, unsure of whether or not I should let myself touch her. By the side of the motel swimming pool my grandmother unpacked her load of coleslaw and pickled tongue while my grandfather disappeared into their room with a full bottle of Scotch. Later we drove to dinner in Joliet, Illinois. In the back seat of my father's car my grandfather opened my grandmother's handbag in search of a tissue, and among the cracked compacts and the crumpled plastic rainhats and the spill of capsules and pills he managed to find a naked razorblade and to cut his finger on it. Without a word he flung open the car door and went off, sulking, for a bandaid, shaming his wife and his son and leaving us to track him in the dense twilight.

Who could follow in the wake of that vacant nerve? Wherever he cast his half-conscious attention, my grandfather remained unsettled. Wherever he went, his indifference to the hurt he had sown—his unseen aftermath—would survive, pristine. And his own unsated hunger: his rash attraction to things, and his abstraction from them; his lumbering urge to move on.

V

I set out with a friend for the Virginia mountains, in quest of signs. I swallow against my filling ears as we make the tight, rising turns on dirt roads, far from the highway. On the second story of Richard's cabin, dull strips litter the floor like blown bicycle tires: copperheads have sought high ground up there to shake off their long, itching hides. I climb the stairs, too, and touch the abandoned skins, hungry to handle the life that was there before us.

Day after day we swing machetes through the underbrush that chokes the yard, and clear the ragged dirt road and edge it with clean stones. Every night while we sleep in Richard's disintegrating shack the order that we have made is undone. When I emerge into the morning sun, still exhausted, I find new growth on the vines and seedlings that we have just cut back, and snakes bloodied in the road where they have stretched out to hoard the last of the day's expiring heat and then been crushed, invisible in the night, by passing cars. Violence presses itself on us; and we are inexplicably, inevitably, of it. At dusk we collect moths and crickets and trap them with wasps in empty peanut butter jars. Voyeurs, accomplices: by the light of burning kerosene we watch them do stumbling battle, down to the last lonesome survivor.

VI

OH BOY reads the rim of my grandfather's sombrero, riding his head like a straw inner tube beside my grandmother's *I LOVE YOU*, in a little black-and-white snapshot—a familiar 2x2 print from my parents' old double-lens reflex—from a Mexican holiday. Their son is *CISCO KID*, their daughter-in-law is *HONEY MOON*, and I am *PANCHO*. We are all perched on a wagon draped with serapes. My grandfather looks half asleep, lounging in his suit and tie; next to him his wife is groping nervously for a place to plant her high heels on the rough platform. My grandparents seem as incongruous here as the *MERRY CHRISTMAS* banner rippling over their heads in a hot breeze. Only my mother and my father face the camera directly. They smile, holding hands. A disembodied arm reaches in an urgent blur from the left side of the picture to steady me as I start to slip off the twitching burro on which I'm saddled. My eyes are closed, I see no one, my parents and my grand-parents levitate silently beneath their roomy, buoyant brims, and I am falling.

PART THREE

"Vulnerable life, that could scar."
                                    —Tillie Olsen,
                                    Tell Me a Riddle

CARS AND DRIVERS

I

On a California freeway my father unveiled his anger for the first time to my mother. They had been married only a few months. His rage shook itself loose—savage and bland as instinct—from the shy, private recklessness of the passion that they'd shared.

Someone cut my father off as he steered down the Pacific coast, on shore leave from a Navy hospital ship at Long Beach. Someone suddenly slipped over the painted white line without bothering to drop a signaling arm out the window—ignoring my father, penetrating his lane.

My father was on him in a second. With my mother beside him he drove his foot to the floor, accelerating without a word. One fender snagging the other, the two cars spun and mercifully skidded onto the shoulder, where they came to a slow, tinny stop, banging gently, then uncoupling.

A door opened cautiously onto the narrow corridor of gravel between the two cars, and the driver stood and straightened his sport jacket. Without even a glance at my father he strode around the front end of my father's car, and bent low to the passenger window. "Never," the man said to my mother, "never let him do that again." And he walked away, leaving her alone with her new husband by the side of the unheeding highway.

II

My mother pops a stick of gum into her mouth and starts chewing as she steers away from the curb—her twenty-year marriage reduced to a last look at the big brick house in the rearview mirror—and begins the long drive with her children to the Wisconsin Dells. We can hear our three suitcases rocking stiffly over the well in the trunk where the spare tire is stowed, our single backup against the wear of miles of rough highway on vulnerable rubber. My mother has stocked a cooler in the back seat with cans of cold pop and with potato chips and Oreo cookies, treats to which she rarely acquiesces in our real life at home.

I keep my sister occupied with license plate games and tic-tac-toe while my mother tries to make her vigil over the car's temperature gauge in the August heat feel like a project that we are undertaking together. I sense my mother's anxiety rising with the needle on the dashboard each time shirtless construction crews wave us down to the low speeds at which the engine eases off in its cooling. The overheating forces her to pull over, and she fumbles with the latch under the hood, draws back on her toes, and strains to catch her balance as a cloud of scorching steam billows out of the radiator. In the stifling breeze my mother lights a cigarette with cupped, shaking hands.

Relieved to be back on the road we regain speed, and corn rises beside us to a height above our heads: the ripe harvest reaching its peak beneath power lines strung from pole to pole, dipping and climbing over the dusty land shaved slowly a million years before by glaciers. We will arrive at our destination, we will swim in the cold resort lakes that the ice carved out. In the pictures that we take turns snapping, my mother and my sister and I are all smiling in the sun. The three of us will head back to where we have come from, past the yellow hazard cones planted at the margins of our lane, floating between the white lines sprayed for miles on the asphalt ahead of us. We want so much to be in motion on the long road, we want to be anywhere but where we really are: on this limping flight from hurt; becalmed together on the striped, turning surface of the earth.

III

My mother cruises from shopping center to shopping center, navigating the mammoth suburban lots, teaching her teenage daughter to drive. As we slowly turn at the end of each crowded row of parked cars, we go on the alert. We peer ahead for the first red hint of a brake light on a reversing vehicle, listening for the cough of an engine starting up, scouting for a chance to dock. This was my mother's idea, a kind offer made to a daughter who's twice failed the parking portion of the Illinois state driver's licensing exam. But now the quest is wearing me down: the memory of humiliation, the lesson that I don't even want, and the squandered concentration; the circling to nothing but an empty spot.

As we make our final exit, my mother flips the windshield visor against the sudden glare—the knife edge of sun unsheathed in the late day—and signals for a left with a faint plastic click. Not far ahead I see a motorcycle bearing down on us, and the helmeted rider, metal and fiberglass teasing the light. Does my mother see that spot on the pavement, I wonder, where we will all collide if she keeps turning? I lean toward her, begin my own hesitant turn, sucked into a deadly geometry: *arc* released slowly into the path of *line*. Already I can feel the force of one massive machine making contact with another. The ugly sounds of steel against steel and of shattering glass are already in the air.

The cyclist touches his bleeding face as he struggles to stand in the street. My mother stares through the windshield, and her head swivels slowly back and forth: first to the now perfectly clear scene of pain that she has caused, and then to her daughter, ashamed, silent witness on the seat beside her.

A cop is standing next to the car, tapping on her window: Open. My mother sees as though for the first time her hands still gripped to the steering wheel, her wrists flexed, poised to make the turn. She makes a barely perceptible gesture of mute explanation in my direction with her head, and she begins to weep.

The cop is leaning through my mother's window, bending to say to her gently: It could have happened to anyone, you were watching for oncoming cars not a motorcycle; this late afternoon light is blinding, you'd be surprised how many drivers have accidents like this one.

Now would be the right moment for me to contribute some comforting words of my own, and I know it. But I am still not ready to forgive—for making me her accomplice in pain, or for being my mother and not knowing what to say.

IV

I start the car and feel for my four wheels, meeting with them the pavement rising and falling beneath me like breath, in and out. It is another August, and the ripe corn is lush and still. Each week the thickening stalks hang more heavy in the heat, cramming the fields, until—one perfect day—the rows melt into a completed, seamless thing. I feel as though I have waited all my life for this moment when it comes: the moment when time yields, and everything that rests on the earth's rough crust is lifted and floated in light.

When I open my eyes I no longer have a steering wheel in my hands, I am no longer holding down a gas pedal with my foot. Beyond the windshield all I can see is sky blue, suspended above, and, cupping me below, cement gray. I tack softly to the right, bringing my mystery car to a halt. To my left the air sags like a velvet curtain, blowing aside with a rush as vehicles speed within feet of me, then settling back into place. I listen from my seat, adjusting slowly to the rhythm of opening and closing, force and deflation, swift *boom* receding to motionless silence; starting to feel a kind of cocooned closeness to the neighbors who pass invisibly nearby.

"Are you alright?" a voice calls thickly, then, as though through deep water, from the opposite direction. A blurred, fleshy disk is flattened to the window. A man helps me to find my eyeglasses in the back seat, and points to the median strip separating the four lanes of traffic where a dark car lies askew, deep in grass. Another figure is swaying nearby. "Drunk as can be!" the man beside me explains as I massage my sore neck. And he tells how it happened: One car speeding heedlessly into the rear of another in the plain light of day, peeling off across the solid yellow line; the other car pitching abruptly forward, then drifting to the margin of the road. He shakes his head: "You were so lucky!"

Five o'clock on a Friday afternoon. My Chevrolet Chevelle, beige and solid, has been brought to an unexpected halt on Iowa Highway 30 bypassing Cedar Rapids. I get out of my car uncertainly on the dirt shoulder, and watch laundry leak piece by piece from my broken, open trunk. My socks are blowing in the gentle wind down the long lane behind my car and into the cornfield nearby.

I can see the road ahead, patches of light flashing on the pavement as clouds slip in and out of the sun's path. I am standing outside myself now, seeing our two shadows lengthen beneath the high, hot sky, a man and a woman, black cut-outs tilting sharply into a lane of traffic where each passing car could mow them down. Dazed survivor, I collect what I can of what is mine and I get back into my bruised car and I drive on.

My father at high school graduation.

MY FATHER, READING

In a photograph from the 1930s my grandfather grins at the camera in a summer-bright outfield. He appears entirely unaware of his son, dawdling in a gray pool of light nearby, unwieldy in the mascot's uniform that he will not grow into for at least another season. My father never stepped out of that shadow, I think; and he remained forever fearful of fading out of view.

He brought his great unease even to books, his plainest pleasure. At a time when the paperback industry was making book ownership a casual event, my father remained insistently loyal to hardcover editions. Anything softer he suspected of flimsiness, of impulse, of impermanence. He devoted hours to shopping for massive bookshelves made from exotic woods and arranging them in our living room, where they lined the walls. When friends innocently asked to borrow his favorite art books, into which Impressionist paintings and Dutch still-lifes had been delicately tipped, my father would stiffen momentarily before agreeing, and he would fret until each one was returned. In grammar school my father gave me a lavish gift edition of *Kon-Tiki*, Thor Heyerdahl's account of crossing the Pacific Ocean on a raft. When I dropped it accidentally in the bathtub, he seemed astonished at my mother's laughter and at the spectacle of the pages bunching and drifting in the soapy water as the book's spine gave way and dropped limply to the bottom.

My father read with ceremonial concentration, nearly always in isolation. His leather chair could be gently adjusted in every direction, but it remained aggressive, immovable in the claims it made to space and to silence. An assortment of gadgets—spring-loaded teak reading trays, the newest light bulbs—came and went, but at the end of every day the book he was reading lay closed at a corner of a small table by my father's chair, his place neatly marked with a leather strip.

My father worked hard to ingrain in my sister and me the same elevated commitment to books. Our family trips to Civil War border states and reconstructed historic villages seemed less like vacations than like rewards for the advance reading we had done at home. (Our single attempt to unwind mindlessly in the Florida sun was a disaster, punctuated from the first day on the beach by my father's ceaseless fidgeting.) We never subscribed to the big picture and news magazines that glowed throughout my childhood on other people's coffee tables, to *Life* or to *Look*, whose spectacular photographs I understood from my father to be lazy substitutes for text. I secretly looked forward to dentist appointments, when I could gorge myself in the waiting room on the glossy magazines in which foot-high images of astronauts and of the Kennedys towered over the print.

Time spent curled up on our neighbors' living room floor with one of the bulky red volumes of the *Encyclopedia Britannica* felt stolen, for my sister and I were actually forbidden to read encyclopedias: unsigned writing was destined, in my father's view, to be superficial, untrustworthy. If we wanted to know about *balloons* we had only to tell him, and he would gladly bring home whole books. But what if we only wanted to browse among things starting with "B"—what if "balloons" hadn't yet crossed our minds?—what if we were simply ready to move on past "A," past "abacus," "anthrax," "astronomy," past *Aztecs?*

*   *   *

In the bright light that sang over our block in summer, lush lawns coasted, cosseted beneath elms and oaks and lindens that reached, nearly touching, across the quiet street. Our new house was more than a vision to my father, though, more than upward mobility. It was an opening up before him of grand possibility, his chance to take the world—solid wood and brick; green growing life—in his own bare hands and to remake it around himself and around his family. He pored over gardening and home decorating manuals, generating plans.

From the backyard I could see my father clinging to the roof, clearing the matted leaves that the house's previous owners had allowed to accumulate in the gutters—scraping away what was wrong, making things perfect. On the most luminous of weekend days, when neighbors floated between one another's yards, half-eaten fruit or sloshing drink or bat and ball in hand, my father would be alone on the roof with a how-to volume that he had picked up in the home improvement section of Krochs & Brentano's, trying to decipher the best way to fix a leak or to insulate against the coming winter. Every so often a dark hunk of rotted leaves would break suddenly free and slide down the roof and the bricks below in a scratchy rush; and sometimes I would hear my father's cordovans skid to a nervous stop at a gutter, and a muttered oath. My mother might turn a cupped hand into the sun and worry aloud about his safety. But when he descended with his book in one hand my father would call out and invite us to look up at his handiwork, to appreciate what he had made happen.

On the weekends that I spent at my cousins' house, knowledge was miraculously liberated from my father's sense of mission and his isolation. In their basement a train set sprawled across the concrete expanse of unfinished floor, and my uncle could usually be found there with one or another of my cousins, testing out a homemade bridge or adding a more complicated switchback. My uncle seemed intrigued by the messy hybrids—half metal, half wood—that emerged from our Erector Sets and Lincoln Logs; and he even seemed to enjoy the acrid aroma of fizzled science experiments, and of airplane cement lingering around the delicate balsa gliders that we spent long afternoons cutting and gluing and then tried out in the yard in the thinning light after dinner. Our curiosity was hardly innocent: following instructions gleaned from library books my cousin Danny and I had connected every room in my aunt and uncle's house with a telegraph system constructed entirely from materials that we had stolen from the local hardware store. Yet our mischief remained, nonetheless, a form of play, rooted in delight and surprise.

*   *   *

My father was a passionate advocate of museums. On Sunday afternoons we drove along the lake shore toward the classical monoliths that clustered around the Chicago Loop.

Just inside the front entrance of the Art Institute he would pause for a portentous moment before taking my sister and me each by the hand, and we would all climb together the long marble staircase to Caillebotte's elegant Paris boulevard under a wet crowd of umbrellas. As we walked the galleries with him, my father frequently reminded us that we were lucky to live in the same city as Georges Seurat's enormous canvas of stippled figures: the lovers and the children and the monkey in La Grande Jatte's sunlight and shadows, the parasols and the bulging bustles of bourgeois ladies enjoying their own Sunday afternoon.

Under unsteady light at the Field Museum of Natural History, papier mâché Indians rode bareback toward campfires around which gaping buffalo carcasses had been pointedly strewn. Everything on display at the museum seemed to me dusty and stale: the Egyptian mummies sealed in stiff bandages, their blackened teeth drawn back into creepy grins; the rough hunks of tree trunk petrified into stone; even the great dinosaurs whose skeletons staggered in the high halls. In the Shedd Aquarium's tanks, though, big, ancient things still lived, stirring up rotted matter as they slowly moved: tortoises, giant squid, garfish. Among the dim, serpentine corridors lined with softly lit glass, strangeness brushed us. As we squinted into the soupy water, a lamprey eel would clamp to the window an open, raw mouthful of sucking teeth—circles upon concentric circles descending deep into a fleshy gullet—or an octopus would press a set of gooey suckers right up to our horrified eyes.

It was the Museum of Science and Industry that remained most charged for my father, most redolent with educational potential. The museum's loudly proclaimed theme was order: technology's victorious harnessing of the natural world to human ingenuity. From behind a long curve of Lake Shore Drive the museum would suddenly appear. We'd mount the stone steps in breathy succession; high above, tremendous columns framed the entrance. Throughout the exhibition halls great machines labored—taken captive whole, transported from far away and displayed alive and intact for our edification.

At one end of the museum a small cable railway descended into the shaft of a model coal mine. A booming pulse simulated the vibrations of mining machinery deep beneath the surface as darkness tightened around us. At the other end of the museum, a low opening gave into the interior of a German submarine captured during World War II. Tight against the curving walls of the sub packed rows of bunks, their blankets and sheets tucked neatly in place. A table was set with napkins and silverware; panels of instrument gauges still blinked brightly, poised to measure depth and pressure and oxygen levels; and switches stood ready to launch torpedoes. To drop soundlessly off the edge of the earth to where the ocean presses every inch of metal with extraordinary force, and to sustain life there for months, my father whispered, bent over us beneath sub's low ceiling—is that not a miracle of human achievement?

Yet I frequently had the sense that unpredictable forces lurked, just barely held in check, in the shadowy reaches of the long corridors where shouts of parents and children constantly echoed. In defiance of my father—emcee of the physical world, eager to initiate his daughters into the beautiful logic of science—much of the museum seemed imbued with mysterious life, tuned to interior rhythms. An electric train looped around an enormous track lined with tiny, stiff shrubs and clumps of miniature houses clustered around platforms and crossings, complete down to the doorknobs and hazard warnings. At regular intervals the train would disappear into a tunnel and then emerge with a metallic, scraping whistle that seemed aimed in some private direction, hardly meant to reach the eager crowds pressing in. Beyond a long hallway filled with the latest farm equipment lay trays of incubating chicken eggs, perpetually hatching new batches of stumbling birds. As I came around a tractor or a combine in the dull, uneven florescence of the hall, a wave of chirping would suddenly surge at me. Ahead, newborn chicks would be uncoiling at the ragged outer edges of split shells, tufts of down flowering softly against the scaly sticks of their legs as they dried for the first time under the hot lights.

My father had little patience for my favorite exhibit, wedged into a corner of an entry hall. According to a posted schedule a vat of liquid nitrogen, condensed from gas by extreme cold, was placed on a small dais. An assortment of familiar objects would be lowered into the vat and then drawn out slowly so that their peculiar transformations could be publicly savored. A red rubber ball would break like glass, instead of bouncing, when it was dropped. A carnation would splinter before us into a thousand wispy shards when its petals were gently stroked. Within the wondering circle huddled there, the world seemed deliberately askew: steam was cold, soft was hard, the elemental turned fugitive. I always lost interest when the speaker began to list the industrial applications of liquid nitrogen; I loved the uselessness of the broken ball and the shattered flower.

*   *   *

I was surely the child of my father's burnished hopefulness: of hope's great appetite for lessons and instruction, and of hope's peculiar expectations and blindness.

My father drafted one of his medical patients to teach me piano, and once a week after school my mother drove me into Dr. Kalman's city neighborhood of brick bungalows and two-family houses. German refugees from the Holocaust, the Kalmans lived in a handful of plain rooms, the entryway lined with a vinyl runner spread over the worn carpet, the furniture covered with clear plastic. The salon was filled nearly to the walls by the baby grand piano. Dr. Kalman and I had to edge in sideways in order to reach the piano bench, and my mother had to wait through the hour in another room. Every lesson made me cry: each time I hit the wrong note Dr. Kalman would bring his fist down on my hand, bruising any finger that got caught over the hard hump of a black key. Yet Mrs. Kalman would always appear cheerfully in the dining room at the end of our session with a precisely arranged tray of ginger cookies and cocoa, and I always complied with the ritual discussion of interesting events from the past week, followed by earnest goodbye kisses. "Now you can tell all your friends that you can play a Bach minuet," Dr. Kalman would say to me at the door, oblivious, as he brought his cheek down to my still teary face.

At home, a white bust of Franz Schubert by the music stand—a birthday gift from the Kalmans—extended my sense of being placed under permanent observation. The browning, shredded Scotch tape that I had hurriedly slapped on the back of Schubert's crumbling hair after an undignified fall reflected the sloppiness that I knew doomed my technique. When my father pressed me to follow my cousin Sarah in taking violin lessons I reluctantly agreed, though not a single sound that came out of that instrument pleased me. (Years later I discovered that my mother had pleaded in secret with my violin teacher to make me quit, because she could not endure my playing; in any case I had long since put a fatal crack in the violin, faking an accident on the basement stairs.) Yet I was still flattered when my father stood by the piano while I practiced or called on me to entertain dinner parties with *Für Elise* or a

Mozart sonata. He'd motion for me to take a bow at the end of each piece, his court musician.

My father turned a corner basement storage area into a home laboratory for the two of us, a snug retreat. He scoured bookstores for biographies of women scientists, especially doctors—Marie Curie, Karen Horney, Elizabeth Blackwell—and for my twelfth birthday he gave me a microscope that I wrapped gently in cotton at the end of each day. He presented me with a rabbit's liver—my first scientific specimen—from the Veterans Administration research lab where he worked after he left private practice, and I filled jars of formaldehyde with grasshoppers that I trapped in the backyard. When my father let me listen to his VA hospital patients breathe through the stethoscope that dangled like a medal around his neck, a muffled wheezing rose toward us as though from deep under water.

My father invited me to help set up an elaborate aquarium in our living room, to bring it to life with him. We brought home clear bags of neon tetras—striped in metallic turquoise and rose, or in yellow—and gently emptied them into the tank. Together we waited for the fish to find their way—slipping through the flaps of plastic, riding water to water. Plants took root in the parti-colored gravel that we spread over the slate floor of the tank, growing so dense that my father had to roll up one of his shirtsleeves and reach down to pull out a handful of shoots from the choked clumps; through the glass and the water he'd wave at me, and his swollen arm loomed like a hairy monster feeling blindly for prey. When I turned off the television before bed I could see the little wet bodies of our fish suspended in the humming fluorescent light and hear the electric pump bubbling and beating, rhythmic as a heart.

I was already sneaking into my father's study to read the *Journal of the American Medical Association* and my father's gastroenterology books, even though flashbacks of naked torsos bulging with tumors frequently kept me up at night. And I was clandestinely dispensing to neighborhood children medical samples that I had discovered in shoeboxes in my parents' closet. Now my father gave me some of his old medical school lab texts to keep in my own room, and he surprised me one night by undraping at my bedside a set of used surgical tools. By myself under the covers, I touched each one. Even in the dark, bereft of their glitter, they seemed resonant, loaded with power being passed, somehow, to me. On a weekend afternoon when he wasn't on call, my father and I laid out the different scalpels on an old table in the basement and dissected a frog together. After we had sliced through the chest my father parted the rubbery skin dramatically with the tips of his fingers and revealed a whole anatomical world. We painstakingly removed the organs, made English and Latin labels, and deposited our collection in small jars which my father reached over my head to place, one by one, on a high, secure shelf.

Once in a while as we worked I could hear my mother, slowed by laundry, making her heavy, careful way down the unlit basement stairs. A coin that had fallen out of someone's pocket would knock loudly in the machine through a wash cycle; or, later, a thick, hot draft from the dryer would suddenly force its way under the crack in the lab door. My father never even looked up. Our work together felt enclosed, hermetic, complete.

*   *   *

Upstairs, my father settled alone into his reading chair. In the evenings he rarely roused himself except to search out more of the cherry pipe tobacco that soaked his corner of the living room in a petulant, unnaturally sweet cloud, or to stare in a daze at the tropical fish in our extravagant tank by the window. And just a few days after my bat mitzvah my parents suddenly announced to their children their intention to divorce and to sell our house. The late afternoon light streaming through the mullioned front windows laid down a row of sharp spears among us.

During our too-long final days in the house the sun was unrelenting, steadily packing the rooms with autumn's last heat. My mother seemed alarmed by the visible way that perspiring jars of mayonnaise and pickle relish on the counter gave up the refrigerator's chill; she moved around the kitchen hesitantly, slowly turning a can opener and loosening lids, dicing celery into tuna salad, unpacking soft slices of white bread from a long, light plastic bag. She'd reach from her stepstool to set a box fan in the window over the sink and aim it directly at the kitchen table; the turning fan filled the close air confined by linoleum and Formica with sound, making it pointless for us to speak. When she dropped into the chair beside mine, delivering our sandwiches to the table, I could feel in my mother a force of disequilibrium. Both of us took our breath in silence, waiting for the briefly refreshing push of moving air that the fan delivered with each pass in our direction, bracing for the stifling lull that followed.

My grandmother cornered me in my room, where no one else could hear us. "Do you still love him?" she hissed; and without waiting for my answer, "how *could* you?" She had made a public ritual of scissoring my father out of all her photographs—scattering glossy slices of his face and of his Navy uniform on the living room carpet around the armchair where she liked to sit. Her coarse cutting left a raw crater in a studio portrait next to which her daughter and her infant granddaughter hung, lopsided. In two trips my father had collected his clothes, leaving a handful of wire hangers dangling on his side of the walk-in closet that he had shared with his wife. Fleeing my grandmother I stood alone on my mother's side of the little room and felt her dresses and blouses swaying at my back, a flimsy curtain unbalanced against the weightless volume left by my father, against his absence.

Our house had been lived in, earlier, by a cartoonist, and throughout the rooms valuable mementos from his colleagues were stored. In her haste to put the pain behind her, my mother simply opened black plastic trash bags and filled them, hardly pausing to look at anything; abandoning the personally inscribed Dick Tracy drawing and the signed first editions of Little Orphan Annie and of The Gumps. But when we flipped the basement light to begin packing down there, we were faced with the wounds that I had restlessly inflicted while life went on, unattending, throughout the rest of the house. Beyond my mother's neat laundry room and the laboratory where my father and I had collected and cataloged, the plaster in the boiler room was pitted from the searches for saltpeter that I'd carried out after reading a book on Revolutionary War military tactics. For years I had been gathering the bound comic strips stored in our attic and defacing the drawings with crayons. And I had enlisted the help of cousins and neighbor kids, gouging rough holes in the life-size Gasoline Alley characters stacked against the wall in the playroom and scribbling with felt tip markers over their eyes and mouths. Near the lab door, the family picnic table was stored on its end, and the frog carcass that my father and I had forgotten was still stapled—emptied, dried out, taut— to the splintering wood where we had cut it open.

*   *   *

Picture us, five years later, at lunch in Manhattan. My father has brought his new bride and his two daughters on his second honeymoon, to show them New York City at Christmas. This morning my father takes me aside on Fifth Avenue and presses ten dollars into my hand. He and his wife would like to be alone for the day. "Take good care of your sister," he tells me, "You're the oldest." The two of us reel along the unfamiliar blocks until I find a window menu in a restaurant across from Central Park that includes items that we recognize. Too late I realize—after we have been ushered into the candlelit room, where the unceasing cacophony of the street is stilled by the blanket of carpet—after Anita has hoisted herself onto a banquette, and ordered and devoured a hamburger and fries and a milkshake—that the great store of cash my father has entrusted to me will barely cover our bill. How could we have used up all that money? I manage to find the street corner where we are supposed to meet my father again, but he and his wife hardly turn from one another under the wreathed traffic light when we rush up. And to my amazement my father quickly takes my account of undeserved luxury as evidence that our time and his money have been well spent, that we have learned an important lesson.

In the evening my sister and I agree to try something else new: ordering Chinese food in our hotel room high above the incandescent city. On the king-size bed Anita lines up cardboard cartons, still loaded with the egg foo young and sweet-and-sour chicken and egg rolls that my father lavishly called for— more than the two of us could ever eat—and she and I experiment with chopsticks, ignoring the stains left by spilled food on the white bedspread shifting beneath our impulsive, clumsy bodies. But as soon as I turn off the lights the TV console shrinks to a shadow and the familiar faces on the screen suddenly seem disembodied and menacing, squawking into the dark. What if we need help, I panic: who can I call? I don't even know the name of our hotel. I lie next to my little sister and keep myself awake as she drifts off, until my father's muffled voice, giggling with his wife, sounds hours later in their room on the other side of the wall.

And picture us at dinner back in Chicago: the indulgent father opening the menu, making an inviting sweep across both pages, encouraging his young daughters to choose boldly, not to hold back, to order à la carte. Avocado salad, squid, ossobucco. Try it, taste it, leave it if you don't like it, order something else. My father's mood rises, inflates, envelops our little table, pronounces us in the midst of a good time. "Like when we all went to New York, when we stayed in that beautiful hotel and you girls splurged on lunch and then ordered in Chinese food."

The steadily diminishing liquid in the bottle next to my father and the thickness of his speech make me afraid to look directly at my sister. Soon my father might knock the wineglass a little too hard with his spoon, repeating a point that we may have missed because we do not seem to be giving him our full attention. Soon our waiter will hear that noise, just a little loud in this elegant restaurant, and return to inquire solicitously if there is anything else we need. Soon the glass will break, bleeding burgundy across the white tablecloth, and we will be leaving the restaurant with barely controlled speed. And soon my father will be riding traffic to the taunting rhythm of red and green lights, silently cutting across lanes without signaling, breathing close on the bumper of the car in front of us, holding down the gap between cars to scary inches.

The silence in the car sucks the air like a hungry, living thing, suspending all of us at the brink of violence. Years later, when she is leaving him, my father's wife will tell me how afraid she was of him and of the ways in which he endangered us. But now she says nothing, and I say nothing either when my father finally brings the car to a halt on the street where we now live with our mother. Through the minute or two that it takes my sister and me to walk up the sidewalk and unlock the front door of the building, to mount the short flight of thinly carpeted stairs to our apartment, I move slowly. I want to speak—to comfort Anita, to ask her if she's OK, if she knows what to do; hungry to make an ally—but I don't know how. I can hear my father pulling away, his tires making a hurting sound.

Who were we to you? Your dinner guests, fumbling with heavy menus. Teacher's pets, your perfect dolls, your always audience; your dream girls, your protegés; your notes in bottles, left to drift back to shore. What you imagined, what you hoped for, what you could never know.

*   *   *

When we visited my father long after we were grown, he would display his shining acquisitions: the handmade, one-of-a-kind coffee table; the first editions that he'd hunted down in a specialty bookshop in a newly fashionable quarter of the city, spread across the table before his daughters. He would speak of new magazine subscriptions—of his discovery of *The New York Review of Books* and of *Antaeus*—with an enthusiasm that projected feverishly his faith in fresh commitments, as though the world's promises to him might yet, somehow, be made good. His wife Dina would serve the meal and he would pour glasses of wine. The dining room steadily heated up and tightened like an inflating balloon as he lectured us on why we should never deface books by writing in the margins. And on one throbbing, bright Sunday when his wife admitted at the dinner table her fondness for the novels of Leon Uris, my father's sense of betrayal brought him to his feet in rage, and he shoved his chair across the room at her.

In the end, books became my father's heartbreak. For most of his last years he could not read at all: in one eye, surgery after surgery failed to repair a detached retina; in the other, an inoperable cataract left him virtually blind. My father clearly saw himself in the classic American writers whose work he hoarded—Melville, Hawthorne, Thoreau: restless, iconoclastic seekers rather than failures—and he loved the compact Modern Library editions that settled them snugly into the palm of his hand. But now the pages hovered out of reach, their print smudged. He strained to sift from behind his clouded eye glimpses of a large print edition of the kind of popular novel that he had once dismissed with contempt.

When I left my father for the last time, after his cancer diagnosis, he lay curled alone in bed against a pillow; his body already looked too empty for death to make a difference. Though he was a doctor, he'd seemed uncomprehending when we had come to him in the hospital: unable to grasp the details of the radiation treatment and chemotherapy that lay ahead. Complaining of a slow leak, he'd fumbled with the spigot and the disposable sac that had replaced his malignant bladder— until suddenly urine squirted, soaking the gown riding up around his hips so that it clung and revealed spitefully.

His marriage was breaking up, and he had reluctantly rented a new apartment. His bookcase and reading chair had, as always, been unpacked first. Mounted on the shelves were the same books: the fat biographies of Churchill and Hitler and Cather; the complete sets of Emerson and of Proust; the histories of World War I, of the Jews, of Western intellectual life. They seemed as loaded as ever with expectation, yet they barely anchored the room. Around the hastily stacked cardboard boxes the smell of disappointment was still fresh.

On a rosewood bookshelf my father had already lined up the matching volumes of Will and Ariel Durant's *Story of Civilization,* a long row of softly colored dust jackets fading into one another. On another shelf he had begun to lay out his Venetian glassware, souvenirs from a vacation with Dina. Beneath a magnifying glass on his reading table a book was jammed open; when I stepped closer a few swollen words shivered in the yawning ring of light. My father had warned us never to leave books like that, and I was surprised that he did not rise, vigilant and fragile, to smooth the bent spine and close the pages.

THE SACRIFICE

In the small Michigan town where he slaughtered animals, my father's grandfather kept his knife sharp as a razor, as smooth as silk, as unblemished as a stone worked for centuries by water. In a single stroke he drew the blade across the throats of cows and lambs, and held their twitching, unconscious bodies until the veins were drained onto the bloody ground. Opening each carcass he exposed the slack lungs, feeling with his eyes and his fingers for deformities and probing with the tip of his blade for the central nerve bundle and the pulsing arteries, the viscous hunks of fat hemming in the liver. For this, hungry Jews paid him: to slaughter flesh and to confirm its fitness to be eaten. To make peace with turbulent, human need; to light ragged hunger with the possibility of repose.

In the days of the ancient Temple in Jerusalem the people drove across the hot, dry plain and up the long mountain the prize fruit of their flocks, their sheep and their goats and their bulls. They entered the holy city and steered their unruly animals along its teetering stone paths, seeking out the great sanctuary with their sacrifices—calling them *korbanot*, the Hebrew word for closeness. One by one the people stepped up to the Tabernacle curtain, where the priest ripped open their turtledoves and pigeons by the wings and laid them on the sticky altar. The tiny hearts still beat there—close to God; as close as blood—until the flesh and the bones sent a redolent smoke upward, sweetly pleasing Heaven.

When my father died, his last wife had him burned. At his funeral a stranger said *Kaddish* for him, stumbling down the

Hebrew page without looking at my father's family. Later, in a public park, my sister and I unpacked a plain cardboard box, the size of a coffee mug, in the unflinching winter light. A mix of powder and rough chunks—bits, unmistakably, of bone— settled as we lifted the plastic bag inside. We let my father's ashes dribble to the earth's surface, onto the dirty snow. And in a minute the stuff was blowing away from us, skipping across the snow's stale crust in a cold wind.

Alone and unanchored beneath the high stars each of us drifts, so far from love's fullness even at the last. Bone of my bone, flesh of my flesh, bearing to the scattered grave earth's skittish legacy: Never enough.

THE UNBINDING

Here is Abraham, yet another man for whom love just wasn't enough. A husband whose wife, ninety years old and long past expectation, couldn't stifle an eerie giggle when she heard the outrageous news of her impending motherhood: unbalanced in her old age by the breach of nature and, perhaps too, by the unanticipated return of hope. A father who named his new baby Yitzchak, for that family legacy of uneasy, skittish laughter.

How could Abraham do it, how could he agree to risk the life of his favorite child, simply to prove something to a voice in the air, full of claims of divinity and extravagant promises for the future? Perhaps that was Abraham's gift: his own kind of hopefulness; his refusal to abide by the terms of the ordinary. Or was he just greedy to be called into intimacy with the transcendent? Maybe Abraham was lonely, and maybe he was tempted by the chance to bind forever what he had come to love most. He surely allowed the dare of "sacrifice" to skate close to the unbearable. And perhaps in risking grief Abraham meant also to call grief close to him, to wave away with feeling's savage clarity the stammering memory of his wife's laughter.

Up they went, then. Father and child, two servants, three days. The ass saddled and loaded, the wood for the burnt offering split, the fire stone packed, and the slaughtering knife. Not another word from God. Abraham led the way up the mountain through an awkward silence that slipped around his shoulders like a badly fitting garment.

His child's innocence would not, Abraham knew, survive this day, and Abraham already felt miserable about his role in its maiming. Seeing the wood and the fire stone, Isaac had inquired about the animal for the sacrificial offering. Abraham's heart shook with his secret. He had explained nothing to his wife Sarah either; this time she would not be likely to laugh, much less to forgive, and Abraham could hardly blame her. Numbly he went on. At the top of the mountain Abraham built an altar and arranged the wood. He called Isaac to him and slowly bound him. He laid the bound child on top of the wood. Trembling, he picked up the knife and began to raise his arm, ready to slaughter his son.

And when it was all over—the risk taken, the test passed, the violence held off, the faith confirmed—Abraham found himself once again alone. Behind him remnants of the ram that he had sacrificed in Isaac's place spit in the fire, and he flicked his hand impatiently to disperse the irritating smoke that trailed his pacing near the altar. There didn't seem to be any point in lingering up there, with the brush tripping him and the voices gone. So he stumbled back down the mountain by himself. Abraham returned without even waiting for Isaac to catch up with him, and he fell at the feet of his waiting servants, exhausted, without a word.

*   *   *

Up on the mountain Isaac shook off the bits of kindling and the dirty leaves that clung to the back of his legs, and massaged the bruises that the ram had left when it burst from the bushes, turning its horns on whatever was in its path, on its way toward death. "Here I am," Isaac remembered his father answering when he'd called out in fear the first time, as they walked together up the mountain path, when Isaac had suddenly done the terrible math: counting the knife and the stone; missing the sacrificial animal.

Here I am? You knew where we were going, what you were going to do, were prepared to do, would not give up doing—for me or for my mother, waiting in your tent, knowing no more than I did—you only knew what you believed you heard in your head, not here, not me, the keening melody of your own yearning to be called to greatness; answered by the ram's horn.

Leave me out of your story: how can you be a patriarch when you are hardly a father?

*   *   *

Abraham lay awake in Beersheba, miles away, sleeplessly replaying the scene. He had not seen Isaac since that day on the *mountain when the angel had called off the killing and then rewarded Abraham for not withholding his terrified son from God. Had he even helped Isaac to untie the knots with which he had bound the boy? Abraham could no longer remember anything except his own relief, and his tumbling, dazzled retreat down the mountain with the angel's promising voice—more power, more territory for Abraham's descendants—echoing in his head.*

I am an old man, and tired, he told himself: do I not have the right to hope? He had passed a long life bound to rough animals, to sheep and oxen, and to the relentless exigencies of water and food in a land where famine could come more than once in a single lifetime. Surely it was not too much to ask of his wife and his son— God had, after all, already agreed—a night of dreaming.

Abraham sat up in bed and looked over at Sarah, sleeping beside him, the wife whose jealousy had exiled his first son Ishmael into the desert with another mother whom he had loved. He had told Sarah that their son was on the road with his servants, following a day or two behind him.

Abraham thought of Isaac, the delight of their last years, on the mountaintop—still bound and waiting?—and he suddenly felt ashamed and sad, an old man, a dreamer and a liar, tired and alone.

*   *   *

You were not here, Abba, when I unbound myself. I worked the knots with my teeth, slowly loosened the cord you used to tie my arms to the cold stone—Abba! Father!—beneath the dry branches, ready for fire.

I know you now, I've seen you suffer and grow confused, an old man wielding a sharp knife and trailing a big idea. I feel sorry for you: you couldn't even manage to hold back from your dreaming what, I know, you really love. I just can't be all yours anymore.

I'm up here in the darkness, I'll find my way back by myself. Don't wait for me, Daddy. When I come down the mountain I will learn how to hold back, how not to need you, how not to let you hurt me.

Here I am, Isaac said out loud finally, unbound and free.

GARDEN DAYS

My grandmother is dying, slowly and without much interest, and my mother and I go to her with freshly laundered towels and sheets. In her front hall is a mahogany coffee table on which our offerings are piling up untouched beneath the boxes of fruit jellies and the jars of pickled herring that her other children and grandchildren have left, trying like us to tempt her to consider life again. My mother drives the city from north to south and back again, riding the curling lip of the lake. Soon my grandmother will be gone and her family will bury her in the cemetery at the edge of the city where she and my grandfather hurriedly bought plots after their first son died in adolescence, of meningitis. But tonight the dark that falls on our way home feels suddenly new—soft—and we roll down the car windows to breathe in with relief the first spring air with its oblivious vitality.

Along the sunless beaches figures quiver in the glow of kerosene lamps, drawing ballooning shadows behind them. "The smelt must be running tonight," my mother says, as much to herself as to me, and she turns quiet, taking the curves in the road with her turquoise Dodge Dart, skimming the shoreline at fifty miles an hour. To one side of us, the city falls away in a blur; to the other side the waters of Lake Michigan, the great inland sea, yield up spawning fish to hands hauling nets in the warm darkness. For a few spring nights the fish are in motion, from the far Canadian border toward these shallows where waves slap gently against the cement breakwater and flicker in the moonlit night.

Men have long gathered here at this time, carrying their lanterns down to the water, to clean and cook their catch and to drink beer. "Sometimes my father and my brother would take me along," my mother tells me suddenly, "and they fried the fish in batter over open fires and served them hot along the piers." Or my grandfather and my uncle would fill buckets with their load of squirming fish and deliver them to my grandmother. Into the night the family would feed at the kitchen table on smelt, small enough to eat whole. They lifted the crisp tails stacked on their plates in grease and coarse bits of kosher salt, and devoured the sweet flesh and the crackling bones before they slept.

*   *   *

On the winter afternoon when my father died, I watched through my sister's picture window the streetlights straining to turn on in the cold air. Snowplows crept down her block in the half light, making a low, moaning scrape as they dragged on ice and on the pavement just beneath the hardened snow. Time itself felt ajar.

After the funeral my sister and my sister's husband and I went through my father's apartment, the emptiness that he had left behind. We tugged, a little fearfully, at the drawers of his desk. Inside one, his checkbook sat on a little box. Flipping through, we could see that my father had just ordered two hundred new checks; in the register he had already recorded his monthly rent and telephone payments. A metal ruler imprinted with the name of a prescription antacid, a promotion from a pharmaceutical company, nested alongside his scissors and a neat cluster of paperclips. My father's milk was still chilling in the refrigerator, stamped with today's date: it had outlived him. The frozen dinners I had bought for him at the supermarket nearby—low-fat lasagna and fish sticks and stuffed green peppers—were stacked where I had left them when I picked him up to go in for surgery.

Belts were draped over wooden hangers in his closet, matched to pairs of pants. Boxes from the dry cleaner were piled on top of one another. We lifted the gray cardboard lids and shook out my father's shirts, starched and pressed: so many different colors and patterns; stripes and plaids and checks. My sister and I unbuttoned our father's shirts and tried them on over our clothes, but when my brother-in-law added the

Burberry's trench coat hanging stiffly in the front closet, still shaped like a body, we suddenly began refolding everything into brown boxes labeled *SHIRTS* and *SHOES* and *SOCKS*. And the clean, stacked underwear that couldn't be saved: I packed his thick cotton briefs, trying not to touch the little pouch creased into the front of each one.

*   *   *

MY MOTHER'S DREAMS FOR ME
1. being happy
2. doing right
3. finding a good job, having enough money
4. getting married, having children
5. becoming what she showed me how to be

MY FATHER'S DREAMS FOR ME
1. becoming a doctor
2. being famous
3. having beautiful things
4. falling in love
5. becoming what he couldn't be

*   *   *

After the divorce my mother rented an apartment a few blocks away from our old house. I could hear my sister's guinea pig at night—consolation prize for the loss of a bedroom of her own—rustling softly in the dark of his cage, knocking food pellets through the metal bars onto the floor of the sunroom where Anita now slept. We had to turn sideways to get there through the apartment's tiny living room, passing tentatively like visitors between my baby grand piano and the sofas that my grandmother salvaged from her house on the South Side of Chicago—to save them, she'd cried, from *goyim*. I took my father's place next to my mother in the synagogue at Rosh Hashana and tried to push away the sense of incompleteness that hung between us like a curtain. The blasts of the New Year's shofar looped unpredictably through the sleek Danish modern sanctuary: raw and rough, like the ram's horn itself; the rusty, ancient call to tribe and to family.

My mother let hope lie fallow, saving for it in secret from her children. But when she was ready, her mind returned to gardens. She would come back to life with her hands in soil, and soil was the joy that came with the plain brick house that she bought, more modest even than the one in which her parents had raised her.

She set to work on the first spring weekend after she moved there, first mowing the wild grass and then rolling an edger down the four sides of green; trimming it to a neat square of lawn, making it hers. She carved a moist black border in the earth for flowerbeds, and she planted what she loved: marigolds and daisies for their brightness; roses for their promise of elegance, their perennial, shameless luxury. A high plank fence straddled the boundary between the grocery store parking lot next door and my mother's backyard, and many mornings splinters of wood poked savagely through holes left by carelessly parking cars, leaving fragile stems and petals crushed on her side in the dirt. Sections of the cheap wood sagged precipitously, falling— flattening, dead weight—across what my mother had labored over, and empty bottles and cans often littered her lawn, tossed in the night by teenagers. She patiently collected the glass and the metal and dropped it into the trashcan behind our patio. She cleared around her injured plants and revived them.

Just across the alley was an empty lot where weeds grew dense and feral. Shards of broken glass and soft booby traps of leavings from neighborhood dogs made it difficult to cut across to the street on the other side without tripping or getting scratched or soiled. But my mother saw something there, disorder waiting for repair—life to be restored. She carried packets of seeds and her garden hose over the gravel and the garbage, and she planted and watered. She drove stakes into the earth and trained peas and green beans to cling to them and grow. She strung white cord from posts to mark her claim, and she tied rags to the cord to ward off marauding birds. The bits of cloth fluttered in whatever breeze caught them as the summer heated up. And soon my mother was loading an old bowl with ripe vegetables, stuffing zucchini with bread crumbs and cream cheese for dinner parties out on her patio, laying tomato slices onto platters where they softened in their own sweet juice next to the oozing, crisp squash.

She joined a local women's bowling league and huddled with her new friends over lamplit scorepads, surrounded in the huge space by the crack and crash of pins being struck and falling. As soon as my mother picked up a bowling ball she would find her focus, first on her thumb and the two fingers that she slid into the smooth holes, then on the triangle of clustered pins at the far end of the long, shiny floor. Sometimes the ball would go straight to its mark and my mother's teammates would clap and cheer, and sometimes the ball would sheer wildly into one of the gutters and her friends would break into loud, comfortable laughter. My mother would turn to them and walk back to where they stood. She moved in small, buoyant steps, almost in slow motion, letting the short distance fall behind her until she was re-absorbed into the waiting circle. After the game she would bring everyone back to her new house and feed them from her garden: plates heaped with fresh lettuce and radishes, plump cherry tomatoes and feathery dill, bright red and as green as life.

I was unnerved by the kohlrabi that my mother brought in from the garden and deposited on the kitchen counter: there was an ugly hybrid quality, something like an animal, about the whiskered bulbs, the living color nearly bleached out from them. But my mother simply cut away the thick outer skin with decisive strokes of her paring knife, and salted the white flesh—her crisp, rugged harvest laid in for the future, for many seasons to come.

*   *   *

The last garden of his life was my father's glory. The spring had been extravagant with heat and sunlight, and the resulting profusion put my father right up, ecstatically, against wildness. That year he printed white labels and mounted them on unvarnished pine dowels throughout the yard. From the patch of patio near his back door he held forth in earth-stained Bermuda shorts to members of local garden clubs. The last of the irises were still blooming in June, feathery, ruffled purple parting to reveal an intense yellow and black heart. Above the low beds of petals—pansies, petunias, impatiens, dianthus— my father had planned out elegant groupings of high stalked flowers in a multitude of colors. Blood orange tulips were planted next to cream daffodils. Rosebushes set pure white against crimson. Close to the ground at the borders of the yard and in the shady rear lay clumps of rich, shiny green groundcover and tiny flowers, each marked with its Latin name: mint *(Mentha)*, myrtle *(Vinca)*; *Pachysandra* and *Hosta lancifolia*. The light, tufted Bachelor's buttons *(Centaurea)* shifted the eye steadily upward to the cool drama of the lilies; ivy *(Hedera)* lent strength against the forces of erosion to what flowered in the air, swaying in the faintest wind. Like the human body, the garden remained a wonder to my physician father, life's order and beauty revealed.

My father loved the living world and its seasons—the visible way growing things are transformed at their time. From the first moist hint of spring he would start to plan, shopping for seeds from stacks of catalogs and preparing the hard ground on his weekends off. On hands and knees he returned to the beds he'd been tending in his backyard, feeling in the brush for what had survived the midwestern winter and for the places where he would have to begin again. When the sun gained enough strength, he would cup new plantings in the palm of his hand and transport them one by one to the freshly opened soil behind his house. He would give each little web of dangling roots a gentle shake, sending a dusty clump of earth flying, before he inserted it into the hole that he'd dug: dirt onto dirt, life to life. With two fingers he tenderly tamped everything down. Every once in a while he would rise slowly, bracing himself with one hand on the ground, and turn a hose to drip onto his limp plants.

On a Sunday near harvest time he used to drive the whole family into the countryside that hugged Chicago's western boundaries. The high, crowded fields of corn rose impenetrably on both sides of the two-lane roads that my father loved for their closeness to the life that we were passing through. Or my father would rent a little cabin for the four of us at a state park, a single room with cots and a bunk bed made up with coarse sheets and thin, scratchy wool blankets. I thrilled to the word *lodge:* the cavernous communal dining room, its exposed log walls hung with deer and moose antlers, seemed to me like time travel, back to the frontier world of the last century that I loved reading about. I always ordered buckwheat pancakes there and lingered over them, sifting the gritty, coarsely milled grain against my teeth. But my father would be eager to get us out into the forest as soon as he had finished his own food. He was roused by that edgy time of year when the trees lose their leaves and the air loses its moisture; when the atmosphere is charged with change. He could hardly keep himself from rushing ahead of us on the trail. The ground was layered with fallen leaves, long turned dark and soggy: they looked like death, my father said, but once winter came they would provide the insulation from cold and ice that mammals in their burrows beneath the surface depend on to stay alive.

The spring before I turned ten we visited Mammoth Cave, where wooden stairs hugging the damp limestone walls led us down from light into darkness; into the dominion of bats flashing in the yellow gleam of our lanterns. Below the earth was a universe worked slowly by water, miraculously echoing the world that we knew from postcards and from our own backyard: delicate gypsum flowers blooming out of rock; "Frozen Niagara," a cavern of stilled, stone sheets dripping over a precipice. Stalagtites and stalagmites groped for one another, and eerie fish—blind for centuries, opaque as plastic—swam in underground lakes invisible from the surface; deep, black waters that connected us to a network webbing the continent. We drove on, another hundred miles, to Cumberland Gap, where Daniel Boone crossed the Appalachians. Just below the pass my father parked the car at a roadside overlook and each of us blew our own breath, white fog on fog, into the low hanging clouds.

My father had believed that he could start from scratch, that he could build from the fresh ground upward. He had thought he could move to a new place and cut back the high weeds, and begin again at the colorless quick. But he was already stuck in time's rut, as surely as the ancient insects that we saw, together, in display cases at the Field Museum of Natural History—gripped in unyielding resin. Once he had unpacked his family in his suburban house he found that the previous owners had painted every wall gray and painted every window shut. It would take months of weekends just to sand and soak down through the layers of wallpaper that entombed each room, to reach the original wood. Out in the trim garage that squatted on the rear boundary of his property, Illinois state license plates were mounted thick along all four walls: a different color for each year, reaching back to before his children were born, to when he himself was just a small child and this house was being built. When he began digging his first garden a discolored ivory chunk emerged suddenly out the dirt: a cow's tooth, or the worn, muddy molar of an ox; leavings of a farm from a century before.

What could my father do, in a world where so much had preceded him, where time was already long and primitive forces still waited in the sea? At high tide on our Florida vacation my parents napped in the easing sun, as the beach narrowed and the families around us began to collect their children and their toys and buckets. When the Portugese men-of-war floated gently in, they glowed, inflated to an unreal blue. I crept close to where they lay in a shallow pool and watched the gummy threads unwind and grope, the rubbery undersides softly pulsing a deep yellow. They lurched on an incoming wave, someone shouted—"Poison!"—and I fell backwards; gulls dipped, shrieking, over me. My father woke and he ran, but it was luck that had saved his little girl. When the next wave took them, my father stood silently and watched the bright crests recede—danger riding, facelessly, the watery surface of the earth. Behind us a man, his skin burnt nearly the hue of his orange trunks, dropped bricks on the taut hulks that the jellyfish left, dead, in the sand. They popped like kids' balloons. In his wake the fragments settled invisibly among the tilted umbrellas. When we unpacked our Florida shells at home— delicately striped bi-valves plucked live from the sucking sand, perfectly marked pairs clamped tight—their dying muscles had let go, leaving barely hinged butterflies, faded and flapping: a sack of stinking flesh that we had to dump outside in the trash.

*　　　　　　*　　　　　　*

By the time I finished Evanston Township High School, human beings had managed to flee their own tired, circling planet into the cushioning silence. And yet infinity continued to drift, inevitably, beyond them. When the Apollo astronauts pulled away from the moon they knew that they had left their footprints behind them, the tread of their bulky boots ground into the dusty soil of the lunar surface. They twisted around for a last look at their long dreamed accomplishment—and saw that the American flag that they'd planted had fallen to the rocky ground. Did they look away from one another as well—cumbersome humans, fathers—as they moved on, and down, swallowing their disappointment, hungry for more of heaven? Far beneath them their own planet turned in the dark, its green mantle of growing things too distant and shadowed to see. And around their hurtling capsule the world hung, *tabula rasa*, airless and empty. I imagine the astronauts strapping themselves in one final time, batting away the bits of scrambled egg and pudding that clogged their capsule after days out of gravity's reach; straining through the chill windows to catch signs of life.

My parents on the water.

Natural History

"First light," they call a telescope's trial run—the moment when the instrument begins to see. Meteorites drop from the sky, delivering hunks of raw material from far away in the galaxy and leaving fresh scars in the earth's crust, the world makes itself new every day. And yet the light that we see for the first time is already old: the light arriving now from the Antannae galaxies started for Earth when the dinosaurs began dying, sixty-five million years ago.

We are all the progeny of motion, descendents of the journey out of fluid. When the tide recedes or the level of the river drops, our unborn young still stand a chance—barricaded seed, in our watertight eggs—against the light and the heat of the sun. While the soft spawn of fish and frogs will die outside water, humans have been freed to roam the wide earth. Yet water remains our life and our history. Traces of the wet that we came from still survive, layered in rock, in the arid places on the planet.

On summer weekends, my parents and I filled plastic bags with fossil ferns returned to the earth's surface by the strip mining operations that my grandfather's company ran before environmental legislation put a stop to the destruction. Steam shovels peeled away the prairie, carving mile-long ditches, probing to the buried seams of coal. In the tons of soil and rock that they scooped out lay the remains of what had grown there. The ovoid stones that we cracked with hammers revealed fine veins and pulpy stalks; when the broken sections lay near enough to one another on the ground we could put them back together like a puzzle. The stems flowed into neat rows of leaves, dragonfly wings stacked virtually intact along a finely drawn line, like a lithograph block. I lay my entire hand over the bits of plants—exactly the size of life—and let my palm rest on the warm rock, molding my own flesh to what was molded there.

The great craters opened by the mining excavations were left to fill in. In the twenty years since the last machine had cut through the earth, water had made the place over. My grandfather would take us out to fish on the new lake in a rented rowboat. Once one of them had steered us out to an isolated spot, my father or my mother would cut the little outboard motor and let me row. In the stillness left by the dying engine, all I could hear was the sound of the oars turning: wood against the metal oarlocks, the splash of broken water, the blades dripping when I paused to breathe.

Thick brush had already grown back over the water's edge, throwing shadows across the ripples set in motion by our oars and our boat. As the sun lifted, my grandfather would strip to his undershirt and my mother and my sister and I would roll up our pants above our knees. We'd all take off our shoes and drink lemonade, barefoot, from the plastic thermos that my mother had filled on the dock before we pushed off for the day. We'd drift through the afternoon, threading live worms bleeding onto hooks and casting our loaded lines out over the water.

And the fish would come to us: bluegills and lake bass, big and beautiful enough to take home and eat. In the silver moment when each one arched out of the water I felt splendidly allied to what lived below the surface. Only then did I remember to begin turning the clicking reel, and feel the force of the fish working against me: the force of old adversaries. Or from the hacked bottom of the lake a catfish would rise to my bait and hang at the end of my pole—ugly, whiskered, horned—as though from a gallows. *Pimelodus catus,* the scavenger brings up from the muck what's been stirred there.

Rock, water—sun, moon, stars—I circle and start, again and again. Scissors, paper—Mommy, Daddy: voracious as hummingbirds, you sought out the sweet, unblemished flowers, feeding deeply as though in a dream, brief as this season's garden. Long as night, bright as day, these things I will remember.

My mother and me, 1953.

(Author photo by Jane Windsor)

Though for the past twenty-five years she has lived in New York City and in rural Vermont, Joanne Jacobson is a child of the Midwest and of suburbia. She grew up in the 1950s and 1960s in Evanston, Illinois, on the lakeshore north of Chicago, the child of children of Jewish immigrants. Her parents bought their first house there, their first garden and front lawn; she rode her first bicycle and learned to drive a car there. Her work as a writer and a teacher is rooted in that America of hope and change, and in the urge to remember.

Her creative nonfiction and her critical essays have appeared in *The Nation, New England Review, Massachusetts Review* and numerous other publications; her book *Authority and Alliance in the Letters of Henry Adams* was published by the University of Wisconsin Press. She has taught American studies, American literature, and creative writing at the University of Iowa; at the University of Angers, France, as a Fulbright lecturer; at Middlebury College; and at Yeshiva University, where she is currently Professor of English and Associate Dean for Academic Affairs at Yeshiva College.